PLAY
YOUR WAY
SANE

PLAY
YOUR WAY
SANE

120 IMPROV-INSPIRED EXERCISES

**TO HELP YOU CALM DOWN, STOP SPIRALING,
AND EMBRACE UNCERTAINTY**

CLAY DRINKO, PhD

TILLER PRESS

NEW YORK   LONDON   TORONTO   SYDNEY   NEW DELHI

TILLER PRESS

An Imprint of Simon & Schuster, Inc.
1230 Avenue of the Americas
New York, NY 10020

First Tiller Press trade paperback edition January 2021

TILLER PRESS and colophon are trademarks of Simon & Schuster, Inc.

For information about special discounts for bulk purchases, please
contact Simon & Schuster Special Sales at 1-866-506-1949
or business@simonandschuster.com.

The Simon & Schuster Speakers Bureau can bring authors to
your live event. For more information or to book an event, contact
the Simon & Schuster Speakers Bureau at 1-866-248-3049 or
visit our website at www.simonspeakers.com.

Interior design by Laura Levatino

Manufactured in the United States of America

3   5   7   9   10   8   6   4   2

Library of Congress Cataloging-in-Publication Data
Names: Drinko, Clay, author.
Title: Play your way sane : 120 improv-inspired exercises to help you calm down,
stop spiraling, and embrace uncertainty / Clay Drinko, Ph.D.
Description: New York : Tiller Press, 2021. | Includes bibliographical references.
Identifiers: LCCN 2020031258 (print) | LCCN 2020031259 (ebook) | ISBN
9781982169220 (paperback) | ISBN 9781982169237 (ebook)
Subjects: LCSH: Self-control. | Positive psychology. | Self-help techniques.
Classification: LCC BF632 .D675 2021 (print) | LCC BF632 (ebook) | DDC 793—dc23
LC record available at https://lccn.loc.gov/2020031258
LC ebook record available at https://lccn.loc.gov/2020031259

ISBN 978-1-9821-6922-0
ISBN 978-1-9821-6923-7 (ebook)

To my mom, Debbie Drinko,
for sparking in me the joy of play.

CONTENTS

Contents

PLAY
YOUR WAY
SANE

INTRODUCTION

I 've got a lot of garbage to worry about.

Like many people, I'm constantly thinking about how I could have said something better, how I could have worked harder or seemed smarter. I spend hours playing out pointless hypotheticals, like what my house will be worth in fifty years if the real estate market appreciates 8 percent annually for the rest of my life. Of course, I plan on moving in less than ten years, and the market is a fickle mistress, so these what-if scenarios probably aren't the best use of my time.

In fact, *all* this garbage that weighs me down—this gray water in my gray matter—is a waste of time. It gets in my way. It prevents me from making connections with others, enjoying the moment, and effectively solving problems. It also drives my therapist crazy. I mean, I'm charming and all, but if you sat through my tenth hypothetical in a one-hour session, you'd be just as fed up as my shrink.

People tell me to "just live in the moment." "Have you tried meditation?" "Forget the shoulda, coulda, wouldas."

But if it were that easy, everyone would be chillin' all day long. You'd treat the loud chewer next to you on the subway with Buddhist indifference. You'd shrug off your partner's nagging. You'd meet your boss's every irrational demand with a calm, yet eager, "no problem, ma'am." After all, why wouldn't you want to restaple five thousand photocopies? It's not like you have better things to do. It's not like she's attacking you personally. I mean, you love thankless and pointless tasks!

This is why we do drugs. It's why we drink. It's why we stare at screens all day. It's why we disengage, why we can't make eye contact anymore. If we were already able to live totally in the moment and let everything roll off our backs, we wouldn't need to numb. We wouldn't need to disengage. You wouldn't have picked up this book, and I wouldn't have written it.

CONFESSIONS
OF AN ANXIOUS AUTHOR

Trust me, I'm no Zen master myself. I'm defensive and angry. I'm stubborn and irritated. I'm embarrassed and shy. I'm selfish and a people pleaser. And worst of all, I'm a total hypocrite. After all, shouldn't I, of all people, know better by now?

You see, I literally wrote the book on living in the moment. After improvising and acting for a decade, I went back to school to get my PhD in drama and theatre studies. I researched and wrote about the science of improvisation, about what happens in your brain while improvising that's different than when you're . . . not. That research became the academic book *Theatrical Improvisation, Consciousness, and Cognition*.

So I'd spent half my life improvising. For years, I researched how people live in the moment. Yet I just couldn't walk the walk offstage. During my research, I interviewed one improviser who described stepping onstage as his "threshold of nervousness"—that is, all his anxieties, worries, and fears melted away as soon as he crossed that line. My threshold of nervousness, anxiety, fear, anger, and worry was also right next to the stage, but no matter how many people I interviewed, or how much I knew about the science of mindfulness, I just couldn't translate that to my day-to-day life.

When I walk in Times Square, I snap at tourists, "Are you walking or shitting your pants?" When my boss tells me she needs to speak with me, I assume I'm going to be fired and plan accordingly. When I fight with my partner, I shut down completely. I hear everything as a personal attack—how imperfect I am, how I've failed everyone.

I clearly have quite the imagination. I'm imagining tourists plotting against me, bosses counting the days until I walk out with my office supplies in a cardboard box, and loved ones drawing up divorce papers.

These are not rational thoughts! They are not coming from my educated, academic brain. They are coming from somewhere deeper and more sinister: my pesky, irrational internal monologue.

I never had these fears onstage, where I always felt creative, present, hopeful, and engaged. Once I cross that threshold, those nasty thoughts just creep away. I get to play with the other people there, look into their eyes, and trust them. I get to listen and be listened to. That internal monologue gets a much-needed time-out.

But what is it about improv that makes my mind more present, that makes me see and listen instead of fear and worry?

IMPROV IS PRETTY FREAKIN' MAGIC

Improv is pretty freakin' magic. There, I said it.

I started improvising on a college team over twenty years ago. I can't believe it's been that long, but time flies when you're playing make-'em-ups for a roomful of drunkards. After I'd learned the basic rules of the art, and gotten comfortable performing, something really strange started happening—I stopped remembering our performances.

I would walk onstage, and then the next thing I was conscious of was taking a bow at the end of the show. I would do an entire hour-long set in some kind of magical fugue state. There is VHS tape evidence that proves I was present, funny, charming, and completely comfortable in my spontaneity during these performances. (Too bad no one has a VCR anymore.)

So what could possibly explain this phenomenon? How could I get out there and suddenly not need to fret or fumble? What made it possible for me to just be?

The secret lies in improv's structure—a set of rules that allows players to stop worrying and second-guessing and to ease into the moment and be completely engaged with their fellow performers.

Think of it like jazz. If each player plays a different time signature and in a different tempo, it's just madness, absolute chaos. It doesn't work. The time signature and tempo are the rules that keep the band together—the foundation upon which beautiful music is built.

Theatrical improvisation needs structure, too. If everyone just went onstage and did whatever they wanted, I don't think many people would want to watch. The rules and goals are the equivalent of time signatures and tempos. Everyone is playing the same game, and, unlike real life, everyone has read the rules ahead of time.

The best-known improv rule is probably "Yes, And," or the rule of agreement. It's a pretty simple concept, really. When one improviser says something, the other one has to go along with it—but also add something else to the scene. Then improviser number one agrees and adds more. A scene is born!

Let's do a for-instance. If player one says, "Mom, I'm home," player two could say, "Welcome back, Chip. Let's see that report card" or "You're back early. I thought school ended at three." Player two should not say, "I'm not your mom!" or "This isn't your house. It's a spaceship." Player one said that player two is the mom, so that's the way it's gotta be. Player one also said that the location is their home, so that's also gotta be.

Lots of people think that conflict is the way to go onstage.

I blame the Kardashians and housewives of various cities for this—not exclusively, of course, but I do think they played some role in our obsession with what I perceive as mindless conflict and conversational volleys that go nowhere.

They're certainly not helping the situation.

Imagine a world where everyone added onto other people's ideas instead of discounting them. Imagine a world where we heard criticism and owned it instead of falling into habitual defensiveness. Imagine a world without the Kardashians! I'm literally giddy thinking about it right now.

Rules like "Yes, And" keep scenes moving and keep people playing the same game. They also help people feel seen and heard. If I know you're going to accept my contribution, I'm more likely to contribute in the first place.

Del Close, cofounder of iO Theater in Chicago, used to tell his students to treat others onstage as "geniuses, poets, and artists."[1] This benevolent mindset prevents people from judging ideas as good or bad. If everyone is a genius, poet, and artist, there are no dumb ideas! (Now I feel bad about my Kardashian comment.)

Oh well. Onward!

Another thing that gets improvisers "out of their heads" is their childlike sense of discovery and play. I take my life way too seriously, and I don't think I'm the only one. I walk past people asking for money as I rush to work. I roll my eyes at the teenage girls laughing about how drunk they were last night. I say things like "But you don't understand what I'm trying to say!" Who says that? People who take themselves too seriously. That's who.

Improv's emphasis on the joy of playful discovery helps me relax and stop being so defensive. Improv scenes continue, even if someone's late. I've never complained about not being understood onstage. I've had pantomimed vacuums become dog leashes and spouses become parents just because my scene partners didn't get what I was going for, and I loved every minute of it. In improv, there is absolute joy found in the disconnects and the discoveries. Nothing is too precious.

The structure and playfulness of improv makes it easier for players to focus on their environment and their fellow players instead of the voice in their head. When you're relying on your scene partner to get through a show, you home in on them. You can't miss all the little gifts they're bringing to the table if you want to build that magical, ephemeral reality with them.

That's what this book is all about. I truly believe we all just want to be seen and heard. In order to feel seen and heard, and therefore valued, we have to learn how to see and hear others—without judgment, and with an unbreakable sense of wonder and curiosity.

I believe that this is the key to unlocking our best selves, and we don't have to be onstage to experience it. We can incorporate play that encourages listening and learning into our everyday lives. And that's exactly what these improv-inspired exercises are for.

12 LESSONS, 10 GAMES IN EACH, 120 WAYS TO PLAY YOUR WAY SANE

Two people hop up onstage. They get a suggestion from the audience, something like "pickles." Then they start talking, pretending they already know each other. Each time they speak, they add new details about their location, relationship, and current situation.

They mime all the props, magically making paper towels, tables, food, and pets appear. Everyone claps and laughs. The improvisers are in the zone, and the audience is riveted.

Granted, improv is not real life, but there are some really important parallels. We improvise most of what we say and do, every day. Hopefully, we listen to and observe the people we interact with, so we react in socially acceptable ways. We may not have to mime furniture, but we do have some control over what realities we're going to create, and with whom.

If you're not feeling that way lately, these exercises can help you regain control—over how you interact with your environment and with other people, how you start your day, and how you think about and move through the world. They're meant to improve your day-to-day existence, just like the improv exercises and games they were inspired by are meant to improve onstage scenes.

So how do these 120 improv-inspired exercises work?

The book is divided into twelve sections. That's ten exercises per section, for all you math whizzes (I just wanted to see if I could say "whizzes" in a book. Turns out, I can.). Each section covers a specific lesson from improvisation. As we go, I'll share some improv rules and concepts to help you relate to and not judge other people, decrease anxiety, and just generally get out of your own way.

We start with setting the stage, just as we would in Improv 101, but this time the stage is the sidewalk, the highway, the office, your house. Shakespeare said that all the world's a stage, and who am I to argue? Lesson 1, Setting the Stage, will help you become more mindful and present, no matter where you are at the moment.

Lesson 2, Calm the Hell Down, is just what it sounds like. Performers can't give their best if they're anxious or upset when they take the stage, and similarly, calming the hell down will help you perform better in your everyday life.

Lesson 3, Finding the Game, will help you bring some fun back into your life. In improv, "finding the game" means looking for fun patterns that can be explored and exaggerated. It's also about approaching scenes with a childlike sense of wonder and adventure.

Lesson 4, Killing Debbie Downer (Getting and Staying Positive), is all about looking on the bright side. Improv demands positivity. If we're thinking about doom and gloom, scenes come to a grinding halt, but if we start seeing glasses half-full, we prime ourselves to be better collaborators and creators.

Lesson 5, Thou Shalt Not Be Judgy, will help you notice when you're being judgmental—and snap out of it. When we're thinking about what's wrong with people, we're missing all the things that are right. This prevents us from making connections, and Lesson 5 will help you turn that right around.

The next lesson is Lesson 6, World of Geniuses. One of the improv mantras is to treat your fellow players like geniuses, poets, and artists. This attitude helps us make each other look good onstage. It's way better than competing, which would make everyone look worse.

Lesson 7 is called Your Mom Was Wrong (You Aren't Special), and I know that might be a tough pill to swallow. But improv works because it's the ultimate team sport. There are no superstars or divas allowed, and Lesson 7 will help you tap into that we're-all-in-this-together spirit.

Next is Lesson 8, Shut Up and Listen. One of the things that improv is really good for is listening, so I've included ten exercises to help you shut out distractions, close your talk hole, and open those ears.

Lesson 9 (Yaaas!) and Lesson 10 (And What?) will help you bring some of improv's "Yes, And" vibe to your daily grind. You'll learn to agree with other people's realities—rather than futilely fighting them—and then add on accordingly.

Lesson 11, Embracing Mistakes, is all about removing the shame and embarrassment that often comes with messing up. The one improv rule that supersedes all others is that there are no mistakes. Instead of letting mistakes ruin everything, you learn to accept them and even integrate them into the show. Lesson 11 will help you do the same in your real life.

Finally, Lesson 12, Shit in the Middle of the Floor (Making

Big Choices), will help you step off the sidelines and start making bigger, bolder, braver choices. Improvisers are (usually) rewarded when they take risks and make big choices, and our final lesson will help you dig deep and start doing the same.

You can work your way straight through the book, trying each exercise in order, or you can skip right to the section that speaks to you loudest. For what it's worth, I've led a lot of workshops on how improv can improve people's everyday lives and strengthen their connections with others, and I always pay very close attention to how each exercise builds off the last. So I've kept that principle here—each exercise builds off the last, and each section is the next logical step in the process, so there is some argument for going in order. It will be more comprehensive, and likely allow you to go deeper into changing some of your bad habits. But if you must blaze your own path, you have my blessing. I mean, it's your book. You bought it. I already cashed the check. So do what you gotta do.

You can also subscribe at www.playyourwaysane.com to play your way through the twelve lessons together. We'll start in January with Lesson 1, Setting the Stage, and end up at Lesson 12, Shit in the Middle of the Floor (Making Big Choices), in December. My apologies; the name of Lesson 12 will make a lot more sense later in the book. Subscribe and you'll also receive an additional improv-inspired exercise each month.

From here on out, I'll usually refer to the 120 improv-inspired exercises as games to remind you that play and playfulness are central to this book. Some games may seem childlike or even absurd at first sight. So don't take any of this too seriously. Improv is supposed to be fun. You're supposed to experiment and make bold choices. That's the best thing you can do for yourself—today, or any day.

Not every game will work for every person. But good news for you: there are 120 of 'em! So chances are, you'll find your fit.

So here we go. Let's play your way sane!

LESSON 1
Setting the Stage

Improv classes and rehearsals often start with a seemingly unremarkable exercise. One grown person tells other grown people to walk around the room. That's pretty much it. Everyone is supposed to walk around and really notice the walls and mirrors and temperature and lighting fixtures. I think it's an amazingly important place to start, really noticing where the heck we are and what's going on around us.

The point is that we don't usually notice our surroundings. We turn streets into war zones and cubicles into prison cells. Noticing where you really are and what surrounds you at any given moment helps you press the reset button. Noticing that a car is a fiberglass go-machine painted cobalt or that your cubicle is actually three short walls with a worn spot in the carpet just below your feet places you back in the real world. No one wants to walk through a war zone only to arrive safely at their prison. We need tricks to press that reset button and see the world as it really is, and that starts with turning our attention outward.

The following are games that help you press that reset button. I, for instance, tend to either walk around in a habitual haze or get stuck in my head and overreact to imagined dangers. These games are designed to help me, and you (I'm a giver, friends), to start noticing the world, snap out of that haze, and start seeing things as they really are. So let's start walking around our metaphorical rehearsal space and really seeing where we are.

Let's set the stage.

GAME 1:
TAKE A HIKE

If I only had to walk around empty rehearsal spaces my whole life, instead of crowded streets and sometimes-hostile offices, I wouldn't be so stressed out. I'd also be penniless, and a recluse, and plausibly in need of a volleyball to talk to and keep me company. Life is not a rehearsal . . . space, but we can borrow a rehearsal exercise and apply it to the places where we do our real-world walking.

This game is deceptively simple. All I ask you to do is walk around your space. That's it. Just walk.

Now, you may be saying to yourself, "I already walk around. This guy's a clown. I want a refund!" To you, sirs and madams, I say take a hike. That's right. Hear me out. Instead of just walking around with metaphorical blinders on all day, I want you to walk around with a completely different mindset. I want you to take a hike and pay attention to everything around you. I want you to start being present.

Next time you walk to the train or your car or to the store, I want you to pretend you're on a hike. Instead of noticing trees and wildlife, you're going to notice, and I mean really notice, your neighbor, their house, the crack in the sidewalk, the way the breeze blows the weeds in your garden.

That weed example reminds me of something very important about this exercise. You must remain detached. This one is so hard for me. When I see a weed blowing around in my yard, I instantly think about how I need to kill it or how many more weeds must be lurking close to the surface or how this one weed is surely lowering my property value. This means I won't be able to sell it when the market takes a dip, and that means I lose everything and will be stuck here eating tuna out of a can for all eternity. In case you can't tell, this is the antithesis of what Take a Hike is all about.

Every time you notice something, you're only allowed to notice more details about it—or you can move on and notice other things. Be detached and impartial. You are a park ranger or a scientographist. Call yourself whatever you like, but I want you to remain observant. Really see and experience the world around you, and stop yourself every time you start spinning your wheels. Started thinking about how that weed will cause you to have to sell your pet dog or move to the desert? That means you're doing it wrong. Just acknowledge that you're spinning, don't beat yourself up, and move on to some other observation.

See? It sounds easy on paper—just walk around. But this can be deceptively difficult when we have become so bored with, familiar with, and judgmental about every little thing in our everyday world. So put on your ranger shoes, walk out your door, and notice what's really out there. No judgment. No future-thinking or spinning. Just take a hike and really see what's out there. You might be surprised.

GAME 2:

TAKE THE LONG-CUT HOME

I find this next game really difficult to start, but as soon as I do it, I feel fantastic. The game is simple: just take a detour while on your way somewhere. Leave early for work, so you can turn left instead of right on Sixth Avenue. On your way home, walk around the lane instead of straight up your driveway. On your way from your car to the mall, walk around Parking Section D instead of going directly into Sears. (Sears is still a thing, right?)

Like I said, this can be really difficult because our brains want us to get the job done immediately. In today's fast-paced world, we tend to have a hard time slowing down, meandering, smelling the roses. This game forces you to stop in your tracks and shift from a future-thinking, goal-oriented mindset to a more immediate state of mind. When you go on a detour, you aren't on your way anywhere. You are pausing your forward momentum, preventing yourself from getting from A to B as quickly and mindlessly as you usually do.

One more word about detours: when you find yourself in the midst of an actual detour, not just Game 2 from this book, I want you to try to handle it with the same aplomb as you do with your on-purpose detours. I want you to enjoy that brief moment in time when you're no longer propelling yourself to the next thing and the next and the next. As you slow down, start to notice how pained, stressed, and generally crazy people around you look when unexpected roadblocks ruin their days. This reinforces the value in slowing down. I don't want to be that guy who yells at the train or hits his fist into his car. So next time a train stops you dead in your tracks, enjoy it. Take advantage. You've just been forced to slow down.

GAME 3:

CALL IT LIKE YOU SEES IT

My favorite way to start a workshop is to have students walk around the space. I tell them to walk with a purpose, but not get caught in a pattern. (For some reason, people tend to just follow each other unless told not to.) Then I tell them to start pointing to objects that they notice and naming them, "Chair! Table! Hat! Tree! Window! Light!" That's the first part of this exercise, and its whole job is to get students out of their heads and into the room.

We miss so much of the world as it passes us by. One way to get out of your head and into the reality of your physical space is to point to things and call them what they are.

As you walk or drive to work or while you're running an errand, I want you to point to things you pass and simply name them, "Sidewalk! Car! Curb! Store! Tree!" I want you to focus only on nonhuman objects for now. Just walk, point, and name. Don't judge either. Avoid adjectives. Instead of "Cracked sidewalk" and "Stinky flower," I want you to stick with only the facts, "Sidewalk" and "Flower." That's all. The reason I want you to hold off on pointing and naming people is that we're just not there yet. I don't want you to get stuck in the bad habit of being judgmental. We'll address this later. I also want to spare you the awkwardness and rudeness of pointing at people and mumbling at them. Do that on your own time.

Now, I do see how pointing and naming could be problematic. People might stare at you and worry about your mental health. You might just feel uncomfortable, which is not my goal here at all. So if physically pointing and naming is too uncomfortable, or you find yourself drawing unwanted attention, you can certainly modify the game and do it only in your head. But if at all possible, throw caution to the wind. Stop caring what people think. Call it like you sees it, and then sees what happens.

GAME 4:

CALL IT LIKE YOU DON'T

Now that you're such an expert at calling it like you sees it, the next step is to get even sillier and call it like you don't. One of my favorite things about improv is the creativity, the nonliteral thinking, the brainstorming aspect. This game should help your brain shake off constrictive and literal thinking and start getting more creative.

The acting exercise that begins with walking around and naming real objects can continue with walking around and calling those same objects very wrong names. For example, I could point to a table and call it a tree or call the window a shoe. We spend so much of our time thinking so literally, so black or white, so right or wrong. I want you to see what it feels like to call things the wrong name.

Start the same way you did with Call It Like You Sees It. Only this time, I want you to point to things you pass and call them the wrong name. Point to a fire hydrant and call it a duck. Point to a crack in the sidewalk and call it a trampoline. But to be clear, the point is not to be creative. I don't want you pausing to think of clever or funny wrong names for things. The point is to just say the first thing that pops in your head. It can be as unfunny as can be. Just keep right on walking and naming, one object after another and another.

Then reflect on what it felt like. I tend to smile and relax a little when I start calling things wrong names. It feels silly and playful to me, maybe a little rebellious. Most of us have to think literally and play by the rules most of the time, so let this game be a little escape, a chance to go against the grain.

GAME 5:

NOPE, TRY SOMETHING ELSE

I feel I've made it pretty clear by now that my mind doesn't always cooperate. Sometimes I think, "You're a dumb-dumb face" when I should be thinking "My my, what a thoroughly compelling and profound statement he just made." Sometimes my mental word stew prevents me from seeing, hearing, and really experiencing the world around me. Other times, it poisons that world completely. I hear my boss say that I'm lazy, when what she really said was that I did 99 percent of my job well. I see an impossible quagmire when there's a completely simple solution. This mainly happens when I try to use computers . . . after 9 p.m. We all have our weaknesses.

So what can we do? How can we try something else? Luckily, our thoughts are fleeting and fairly mutable. They can change. We just have to retrain ourselves to try something else, something better.

The next time you catch yourself judging others, being critical or negative, complaining or fretting, or just generally thinking crappy thoughts, I want you to catch yourself red-handed. Then say, "Nope, try something else." Instead of saying, "This bar is so loud. I hate that noisy table," replace that thought with the next thing that comes to mind. "I like guacamole." Not all thoughts have to be profound. The world would be pretty boring if we only thought about Nietzsche and hermeneutic circles. And besides, sometimes the guacamole is just too good to not think about.

If your next thought is still no good, try another one. And another and another. Keep telling yourself, "Nope, try something else," until you land on a thought worth keeping. Recognizing when our thoughts are not what we want in that moment is half the battle. The rest of the fight is about resetting our habitual thinking.

I think you'll find out fairly quickly that with some practice, you can think hundreds of thoughts in rapid succession. Once you start to see the many possibilities, I think you'll start landing on fewer crappy thoughts. And that's a big step toward living a calmer, more content, less crappy existence.

GAME 6:

A MUSEUM IS JUST A STORE WHERE YOU CAN'T BUY ALL THE THINGS

I don't like to go to museums. I know, I know—I'm supposed to love them. Going to museums demonstrates how smart and curious about the world you are, but I'm just not that into them.

So I came up with a solution. When I do go to a museum, I pretend I'm shopping. (I guess the irony there is that I also strongly dislike shopping.) Anyway, in each new room of the museum, I play this game where I have to walk around and choose one thing I want to buy and identify a rationale for why. It's a fun game to play with friends. It gets you talking about preferences and art and junk, and it forces you to slow down and look at that art instead of feeling crowded and stressed out.

Why not take the museum game to the streets, to the office, to any place where you need to slow down and enjoy the moment? Next time you're overwhelmed in a crowd or by your anxious thoughts, go pretend shopping. Do you want to buy the pencil sharpener or the Ikea art? Do you want to buy the fire hydrant or the squirrel eating a nut while sitting on said hydrant? Think about why. This way you stop those pesky unpleasant thoughts, start noticing the actual details in the world around you, and shift your thoughts from internal worry to outernal (that should so be a word) wonder. The other great thing here is that you're focusing on the thing you like and not the one you hate. That's helpful to shift into a more positive mindset, something we'll be working on later.

And don't tell anyone about how I don't like museums. That can be our little secret.

GAME 7:

SHAKE IT OFF

I'm almost embarrassed to include this next game. It seems so obvious, but it always does the trick for me. It's right there in line with the "stop and count to ten" method. You know, someone says something to make you mad. Then that same irritating person tells you that you look upset and that you should "just breathe" or "count to ten," and then you want more than ever to crush that person with your bare hands? Yeah, me too.

So counting to ten doesn't work so well for me. There's nothing worse than being told to calm down when you're upset. Feelings are feelings, and if we could just will them to change, we would probably just do that. So before someone can tell you to count or breathe, just shake it off.

During improv rehearsals, feelings can start to accumulate. People start feeling stressed out or exposed or ashamed or angry or frustrated. Lots of feelings are being explored during a good rehearsal. In order to reset, improvisers tend to just shake it off.

To shake it off, you shake everything—your head, arms, feet, and legs. It's also especially effective to hop around a little and make that horse-neighing sound with your lips. Does that sound have a word? *Plrhplrhplrh?* Whatever that noise is when you loosen your tongue and lips and blow out, letting them vibrate.

This distracts your mind by getting the body moving, and the horse sound helps release some of the built-up pressure. It's like pressing the reset button. I think it's especially awesome because it's so silly. When I count to ten, I calmly think about how angry I still am for ten long seconds. (What can I say? I'm really stubborn.) But when I hop around and exhale air and wiggle my whole body, it becomes extremely challenging for me to hold on to negative thoughts.

So try it. Hop, jump, wiggle, and neigh. Just shake it off. I mean, if it's good enough for T. Swizzle . . .

GAME 8:

REPEAT AFTER YOU (MANTRA)

This next game isn't improv-specific. You just repeat something over and over in your head. This, at the very least, gives your squirrel brain something to focus on, and as you'll see in later games, you can really choose your own adventure as to what mantra you want on repeat in your skull-place.

You can choose any phrase to think over and over, but I suggest something fairly positive, since we're just beginning. Please don't choose "I hate the world" or "Everyone is the worst." Actually, you may already be thinking those things. Instead, take control. Choose something very specific and stick with it. Then see what happens. I'm thinking something like "What a nice day" or "I got this."

What always happens to me is that I lose my mantra. Someone cuts in front of me, and my "I love everything" quickly turns into "I will seek and destroy you, you dumb face." That's normal. That's totally okay, isn't it? I hope so, but I'll for sure ask my therapist. Either way, each interruption is just a perfect little moment to remind yourself of your mantra instead of letting the buzz-killing moment hijack it. Just pause. Remind. And get the original, positive mantra churning again.

Keep experimenting with different mantras. Sometimes corny works for the cool, and sappy works for the stoic. You won't know until you try. Just keep track of what's working. What's making you feel lighter, more present, and just generally less irritable. You know, not wanting to seek and destroy dumb faces quite so much.

GAME 9:

GOOD TOUCH

As we get older, it's increasingly more discouraged for us to touch everything, slobber on stuff, and put everything in our mouths. (I mean, depending on your social milieu.) But babies are learning so much so fast, they're notoriously in the moment. Learn from the wisdom of the diapered. Slow down and start touching stuff again!

Now I know there's always a wise guy out there who's apt to bend the spirit of this game into something more sordid. Stop right there, wise guy. This game applies only to inanimate objects. Plants, if you must. No people touching. It had to be said. Plus, we'll get to healthy human interactions later in this book.

I'm talking about stopping and touching the roses. Not the thorns. Common sense, people. Stop and touch a tree, the fence, the table, napkins, and windows. Things other than your phone and credit cards.

It doesn't have to be gratuitous. You don't have to go on a touching rampage. Just notice objects and touch one every now and again. And really note all the details about how that thing looks, smells, and feels.

It's hard to interact in a world we're not noticing. Start setting the stage for later games now by slowing down and truly seeing, feeling, and hearing what's already going on all around you.

GAME 10:

SCHEDULE YOUR MONK TIME

I put a lot of stuff in my day planner, from walking the dog to picking up dry cleaning to finishing a long-term work project. I focus a lot of my mental energy on what I have yet to achieve and what I hope to complete. This is future thinking, and it keeps me from living in the moment, but we have to keep track of all the things we need to do in a day, right? I'm not twenty anymore, so if I don't focus my energy on my future errands and write that shit down, I will most likely forget. Then I'll be living in the past, regretting making the big mistake of not having a to-do list, an equally not-in-the-moment mode of thought.

So I'm not asking you to drop the to-do list. I would never dream of doing that myself. All I'm asking is that you schedule in your mindfulness, schedule in your monk time.

I simply write "Be" on a separate line in my to-do list. I make sure to look at it every day. I try to complete it as often as I can. It's just a reminder to be present to my friends, family, and acquaintances. It's a reminder to look at the world around me as it really is, without judgment and without defensiveness, just to take it all in and enjoy the moment. That simple little "Be" reminds me to stop planning the future and worrying about the past.

You can pick any word or phrase that works for you. Add it to your to-do list. Remind yourself to stop and enjoy the world as it really is. And the more you obsessively check your to-do list, the more you'll be reminded to stop worrying and just be.

Now that you're feeling more mindful and connected, let's talk about some ways you can calm the hell down.

TIME-OUT:
LET'S TALK ABOUT YOU

This is the first of four Time-Outs that will appear throughout the lessons. It's my way of Zach Morrising you. I want time to stand still, so we can talk face-to-face, just you and me.

This Time-Out is about you getting the quality alone time you need to recharge your battery. In order to have a clear head for these games, you're going to need some downtime, some time without other people pestering you.

Some people meditate. There are great apps that can help if you go this route. My brain is always on the go, so I struggle with meditation if I don't use the apps. I need a guided meditation to let my thoughts go. It also helps me to imagine that my thoughts are clouds. I'm not forcing them to stop; that only causes more thoughts. I'm just observing them as they roll on by.

You can also take walks alone, or be all "Calgon, take me away" and take a bubble bath with some scented candles around the tub.

It doesn't matter how you get your alone time, just that you're getting it.

I'm glad we had our little talk.

Now, please proceed.

LESSON 2
Calm the Hell Down

Now that you've set the stage, I hope you're feeling a little more mindful, a little more plugged in and connected to the world around you.

Phase two is all about calming the hell down. Before we're ready to become more positive, less anxious, and more playful, we first need to take a few breaths and just practice relaxing. Easier said than done, right?

We live in a society that celebrates type A, go-go, never-stop, hard-work-all-the-time grinding. I'm a Midwestern, corn-fed guy, so I'm a big fan of a strong work ethic. But as in all things, moderation is crucial.

What's the point of grinding when life seems to pass us by? When we're too anxious and stressed out to enjoy the fruits of our labor?

Take another lesson from improv. Improvisers warm up before a performance. Part of the warm-up is about getting their energy up, connecting with teammates, and getting their brains primed for creativity, but another equally important part is straight up chillin' the hell out.

It's much easier to connect with others, focus, and come up with ideas when we're in a calmer mental state.

Improvisers might close their eyes and count to twenty as a group or do some light stretching to calm and center themselves.

Being stressed out and just generally agitated is not going to make for a good performance. So actors and improvisers do what they have to do to make sure they calm the hell down.

So should you.

I know I carry around a lot of stress and tension. Just this morning my dog shat on the dining room rug. Then my toddler shat in her pants. Then I dropped her at daycare, where she peed in her pants.

I think you can see a pattern emerging here. Now I'm hiding in our home office while ten men loudly argue over how to put our new air ducts in correctly.

Stressful.

So we all have to learn a lesson from improv. We all have to learn how to calm the hell down.

Now, I take yoga classes and try to meditate here and there. I also go on walks and try to remind myself to calm down throughout an average day.

But these games are an extra sprinkle on top of whatever you're already doing.

There are some visualization exercises and some breathing exercises in addition to the improv-inspired ones, but they're all here to help you relax so you can eventually start connecting, creating, and turning up the joy in your life.

Now take a deep breath, and . . . calm the hell down with me.

GAME 11:

TRACE YOUR HAND

My daughter likes to trace her hand. Doesn't matter if she's using a colored pencil, marker, or crayon. She loves tracing that tiny toddler hand.

This exercise is as simple as tracing . . . and breathing.

Hold one hand out with your fingers outstretched.

Your index finger on the other hand is going to be the tracer.

Start at the outside base of your thumb, and breathe in as you trace up to the top of the thumb.

Breathe out as you trace down the inside edge of your thumb. Then in as you trace up your index finger. And on and on until you trace around your whole hand.

Hold on. I'm gonna try it right now and let you know how it goes . . .

. . .

. . . Okay, done.

I have a few notes.

- The feeling of tracing is nice. Focus on this feeling and your breath as you trace your hand.
- I found closing my eyes to be helpful. It made me feel more relaxed, which is the whole point.
- Take your time. This is definitely not a race, so avoid the impulse to try to "just get it done."

Happy tracing!

GAME 12:

NOSTRIL PARTY

It's time for a nostril party!

I stole this next exercise from my yoga classes. After a long hiatus, I'm doing yoga again. It's the total package: exercise, stretching, meditation.

But it's also full of fun breathing exercises like the one I've renamed Nostril Party.

This is another simple one. Just place your thumb on one nostril and the middle finger of the same hand on the other nostril. Then press one nostril closed while you breathe out and in. Then switch to the other nostril and breathe out and then in with your other nostril.

That's the cycle. Out, in, switch, out, in, switch.

I like to go really slowly and pause after every single breath.

Just like with Trace Your Hand, the feeling of my finger and thumb on my nose gives me something to focus on. The added bonus with Nostril Party is that it forces you to use both sides of your nose. This is great for getting oxygen into both sides of your brain.

Just make sure to clear those bats out of the cave. And this isn't the best game when you have a cold.

I even have a pretty severe deviated septum from a modern dance mishap, but I still find that Nostril Party helps me circulate air better and get things flowing through my powered-down nostril.

Bonus points if you play this game in public. One point for every cycle.

Now that's a party.

GAME 13:

BIRTHDAY CAKE HANDS

It's time for our third and final breathing exercise. And it's a party . . . a birthday party!

If you're feeling stressed out or just generally not chill, Birthday Cake Hands is a quick way to catch your breath and calm the hell down.

Just hold your fingers in front of you like they're make-pretend birthday candles and it's your make-pretend birthday. Close your eyes, make a wish, and then blow one of your "birthday candles" out. With a slow, powerful exhale, blow on one finger and then put that finger down as if it's a flame that's been extinguished.

Then take a slow, deep breath in and repeat on another finger.

You win this game by making five wishes and blowing out five "birthday candles." Because, once again, winning is about being able to calm the hell down more than it is about having our wishes granted.

And if you're still stressing after your five wishes, just whip out your other birthday-cake hand and blow out five more candles.

GAME 14:

COUNT TO 10 . . . OR 100

There's an acting exercise where everyone closes their eyes and takes turns as the group counts to twenty. I'm making it sound dumb, but it's a great exercise. You have to take turns saying the numbers, but you can't go in a set order. You say the next number when you feel the urge to. If more than one person says a number at the same time, you start over.

It's fun times and forces everyone to slow down, listen, and take their time. So I wanted to adapt this for a party of one, a party of just you.

When you're feeling stressed or antsy or agitated, close your eyes and start counting. Don't rush it. You should only say the next number when you "feel the impulse." Whatever that means for you.

Count to ten this way. Or twenty. Or even a hundred if you're feeling really rough.

GAME 15:

YOU ON A BEACH

I don't know about you, but I like to be on a beach. A lot. I really like being on beaches.

This game comes from my love of beaches and my time training at the Strasberg Institute. It's a famous acting school known for churning out thespian greats like Laura Dern, Marilyn Monroe, Scarlett Johansson, Barbra Streisand, and . . . me.

Strasberg is famous for Method acting, which many people confuse for losing a hundred pounds or locking yourself in a dark room to get into character. That's not really the point of it, but the point of me even mentioning it is that I also stole some fun acting exercises from my time there.

Like You on a Beach.

If you were taking classes at Strasberg, they might call this "Warm Sun" or "Sense Memory."[1] For my version of this exercise, you need to take some calming breaths and close your eyes. Then try your damndest to imagine that you're on a beach.

Try to visualize with all five senses. See the horizon. Hear the waves. Smell and taste the salty mist from the ocean. Feel the sand between your toes.

Now, some people are better at visualization than others, but the point isn't necessarily that you successfully picture being on a beach. The point is to calm the hell down, which pretending to be on a beach always does for me.

After all, you may not actually *be* Laura Dern, but you might as well act like it.

GAME 16:

QUARANTINE SCENE

The name of this next game was a lot funnier before March of 2020, but I still stand by it.

For Quarantine Scene, you need to set a timer and force yourself to take a break.

Let's say your kids are screaming or your husband is on your last nerve. Instead of doubling down and muscling through, stop.

Set a timer for five minutes . . . ten minutes . . . *thirty* minutes if current stress levels demand.

Then take a bath or read a book or go for a walk or watch the grass grow. Do something that helps you relax and calm the hell down.

Your family will thank you.

GAME 17:

RELAX-ATHON

Sometimes I look around and see people just living their best lives. They look calm and stress-free. Meanwhile, I'm running around like a chicken with a lot on his to-do list and not enough coping mechanisms to handle it well.

Isn't that how the saying goes?

Well, if you can't beat 'em, join 'em. The next time you're ramping up, I want you to make relaxation a competition. Play to your strengths. If you're a competitive type A type, relax to win!

Look around at all those chill people, and then do what they do. Chill. Then try to chill more than them. Pay attention to their breathing and posture. How do chill people move and interact with others? Then do the hell out of those things.

And even if you don't win the Relax-athon, at least you'll kind of win at life because if being stressed out is losing, calming the hell down has to be winning.

GAME 18:

OM NO SHE DIDN'T

I always get embarrassed when I have to say "Ommm" during a yoga class. I'm usually the only man, and—ask any of my students—my voice has a tendency to crack even though I'm well past puberty.

I'm asking you to push through any embarrassment or shyness, and "Ommm" anyway.

I'm also asking you to Om outside of yoga class. This shit is getting real!

When we say Om, we're starting with a round sound and slowly ending with a humming sound. This evokes a sense of infinity. Like your one little Om is reverberating out in the universe for ever and ever.

It's also super-relaxing to Om. So let's Om, shall we?

For this game, you need to Om at least three times any time you get stressed out or worked up.

Extra points if you do it in public.

Extra extra points if you do it right in front of the person who is stressing you out in the first place.

Because nothing says "Get out of my face" like an "Om shanti shanti."

Om, Felicia.

GAME 19:

SENSE MEMORY CIGARETTES

I'm borrowing from Strasberg again for this exercise.[2] Maybe because I miss doing sense memory work. Maybe because I really *do* want to be Laura Dern.

But that's neither here nor there.

I'm definitely not advocating smoking. In fact, I think it's a really bad scene, and I told my husband when we started dating that if we ever had kids, he would have to stop smoking.

Spoiler alert: He stopped smoking.

But even though I'm anti–real smoking, I'm not at all above pretend-smoking.

Sometimes when I get worked up or pissed off, I take a pretend-drag on a pretend-cigarette. And strangely, I feel a lot better.

That's what I want you to try.

Someone pisses you off? Take one pretend-puff.

Someone makes you want to burn down their house? You'd better smoke an entire pretend-cigarette.

The good news with pretend-cigarettes is that they don't cause lung disease and can't be used to burn down houses.

Plus, slowing down and deepening your breathing will help you calm the hell down.

GAME 20:

SURFER DUDE

I think we've established that I'm not a relaxed person. It's pretty clear by now that I also have no chill.

When they were doling out chill, they for sure ran out before my name was drawn.

So I look at stoners and surfer dudes with envy. They seem so relaxed. Even when they run out of weed or get bitten by sharks, they're way more chill than me on a regular Clay day.

So for this exercise, just pretend you're a stoner or surfer dude.

Your coworker is pressuring you to turn in your report? "Totally cool, man. I'm totally working on it, dude."

Your kids are screaming at each other and also at you? "Chill, man. Y'all need to totally take a chill pill, man. You're killin' my vibe."

You get the idea. We're not going for Oscar nominations here. We're just trying to slow down our cadence and embody a more chill vibe.

Because if you don't have much chill, you can at least pretend to be someone who does.

And just like that, we've worked our way through ten improv-inspired exercises to help calm the hell down. Hopefully, you're feeling more mindful and relaxed, because now it's time to start finding the fun.

LESSON 3

Finding the Game

When an improviser gets onstage, they're looking for fun. It's basically the polar opposite of how I leave my house each morning. I'm ready to do battle! I'm ready to scowl at the car that speeds into the crosswalk. I'm ready to yell "Excuse me!" to the woman taking up the entire sidewalk because she's staring into the oblivion of her smartphone. I'm ready to use my stroller as a weapon of mass destruction.

But believe it or not, there is another way. We can leave our houses every morning ready to find the fun, ready to make a game of what's happening all around us.

What does it mean to find the game? It means looking for what's fun or funny in any given moment or situation. Think about little kids. Life hasn't beaten them down yet, so they see the fun and the funny in things all the time. They notice the game.

If you walk back and forth between two rooms a couple times, your baby thinks that shit is a game! She is playing peekaboo like her life depends on it. She is laughing and clapping because she found the game.

Rediscover your inner baby. Start retraining yourself to find those games.

Let's get started.

GAME 21:

SIDEWALK BOMBS

I grew up on a farm, and life on a farm can be . . . simple. My parents weren't shuttling me from ballet to soccer to tutoring. We got locked out of the house in the morning, we'd find peanut butter sandwiches on the porch around noon, and then Mom would ring the dinner bell around six, meaning we were finally allowed to reenter the house.

There weren't preplanned activities for us to do out there on the farm. We had to find the game! We made forts and climbed trees and pretended to be characters from our favorite movies. I was the android from *Aliens* one summer, and I still think that performance resonates with the groundhogs and rabbits who skittered by as we played our faces off.

One of the games born of this forced creativity was Sidewalk Bombs. If I was walking, and I didn't really want to be locomoting in that particular way to get to that particular place, I would motivate myself by pretending bombs were going off behind me.

Sounds insane, but nothing motivates you to pick up the pace like thinking the sidewalk will explode and kill you!

So as you walk or drive to work or to pick up the kids or run errands, imagine that the ground where you are is wired with explosives. Then set a time and a goal destination. You might think, "Okay, I have to get to Exit 14 in ten seconds or the bomb will destroy me!"

Then you count down and play out the scenario. The fun thing here is that you don't die! If the bomb gets you, just make a sad face and play again. If you beat the bomb, well, good on you.

This is a close cousin of the Lava Game, when kids pretend the floor is slowly filling with lava, so they have to jump up on the sofa or coffee table to not become incinerated. It's a way to take the ordinary—your commute—and make it extraordinary. After all, your make-pretend life depends on it.

GAME 22:

HELICOPTERS FILLED WITH CASH

Improvisers pay attention. And then they turn what they notice into comedy gold. You don't need to do that second part, but I do recommend opening your eyes and having a little fun with your imagination.

Planes and helicopters fly over our heads every day, but we tend to pay them no mind. For this game, all you have to do is start paying them mind and pretending they're going to pay your mortgage.

Every time a plane or helicopter flies overhead, I want you to imagine that it's filled with cash. Imagine it drops the cash, and it flutters over to wherever you happen to be. That's it. That's the whole game. Pretend air traffic is making it rain cash money . . . on your head.

It's all about turning the ordinary into something extraordinary, making the familiar novel.

Plus, swimming in cash, even imaginary cash, is better than zoning out or cursing someone out. Am I right, ladies?

GAME 23:

ARE YOU MY MOTHER?

Here comes another game born from my boring farm childhood.

Sometimes my mom would leave us kids in the car while she went into the grocery store. (Don't worry, we weren't babies. I suppose we were old enough to open the car door should the heat inside become unbearable. I don't think our lives were in danger, but I digress.) The point is the magical way we passed the time while waiting for Mama to come back out with the groceries.

We would take turns saying, "All right, the next person to come out of the store is your mom." And then hilarity ensued!

Sometimes a burly trucker would end up being my sister's mom or a little old lady might be my mom. I didn't say the game was sophisticated or mature, but it did its job. It served its purpose. Our game entertained us by making us really pay attention to something, in this case: the people exiting the grocery store.

So the next time you're waiting, tell yourself that the next person to round the corner or enter the coffee shop is your mom or brother or girlfriend or nemesis.

It will force you to be more present, opening your eyes to what's going on around you—and *who's* going on around you.

Plus, it's kinda funny.

GAME 24:

ALIEN GAME

Anyone who knows me knows that I boil in a simmering rage anytime I'm in a crowd. I think there are a lot of people like me. (At least, that's what I tell myself.)

The reason for my freak-outs is simple. I can't control how I will get from point A to point B when I'm in a crowd. I can't walk as fast as I'd like or on the part of the sidewalk I want. Juggling so many other people's expectations puts a major monkey wrench in my plans. Then I start trying to guess where people will walk, and it just gets messy. I stop. I switch directions. I huffle, I puffle.

I'm painting myself out to be a major wackadoo, but only to let you know you're not the only one. There is hope for all of us.

You just have to change your expectations. Or, more precisely, you have to get rid of your preconceived notions about people altogether.

Pretend you're a damn alien. Sent from another planet. You don't know how Earth people maneuver. You don't know where they're going or why. The best you can do is watch the Earthlings carefully and try to do exactly what they do. After all, you don't want to stand out.

If someone is walking very slowly, do the same. Try to find the median flow of the group. You want to be as average a fake Earthling as possible.

This will stop you from getting caught up in how *you* want to walk and help you blend better into the flow of what's already going on. Stop fighting it.

This will also work for all you road ragers out there. Let's suspend disbelief and say you're an alien who came to Earth already knowing how to drive Earth's primitive automobiles. Go with the flow of traffic, instead of fighting it.

After all, we do come in peace, don't we?

GAME 25:

RED CAR

Driving is one time—not the only time, but one time—that I forget to pay attention to what's going on around me. There have been more than a handful of times that I took a wrong turn because I absolutely wasn't paying any attention to what I was doing. This all ends with the Red Car game.

It's painfully simple, almost like the Alphabet Game on a road trip. But what it does is force you to pay more attention to your surroundings.

Just count every red car that you see. Simple. You can set a time limit and a number goal. For example, you might say, "If I see three red cars in the next two minutes, I'm the best person in the world" or "If I count five red cars in ten minutes, I win a million dollars."

Obviously you don't really win anything, but that's not super-important. The important part here is that you stopped thinking about that nine o'clock meeting or how your husband would be perfect if only he would take out the garbage without you asking every time.

Simply counting cars can get you out of your own head and into the world around you. And it can also win you a cool (fake) mil.

GAME 26:

SECRET WORD

Like so many of the games in this book, this one comes from someone else. Yeah, I stole it. I'm from the *Pee-wee's Playhouse* generation, and I think there's something really solid about the secret word. You see, on *Pee-wee's Playhouse*, whenever anyone said the secret word of the day, everyone at home needed to "scream real loud!"

I'm not suggesting you go around screaming when people say your secret word of the day, but I do want you to choose a word and then note, simply by smiling, every time it's said. Extra points for screaming. Actually, wait. I take that back. I don't think it's a great idea to run around screaming like some rando. You better just smile.

Like most of the games in this lesson, it's about finding the game, but also about paying more attention to the world around you. Thousands of words fly in one ear and out the other as we bustle through our days. This game lets you savor just one of those words each day.

Now, that is something that should *actually* make you scream real loud.

GAME 27:

DANCE BREAK

I'm not gonna lie. This game got me through my doctoral program. And college. And the writing of this book.

It couldn't be more simple. Don't put this in your day planner, but at some point in your day, drop everything and dance. You can use music or not. You can be alone or not. You can be eating frozen yogurt simultaneously or not. You get the idea.

We lose our connection with our bodies by sitting and talking and thinking all day. This is a trap. Like Lady Gaga once said, "Just Dance." And speaking of "Just Dance," I would be remiss if I didn't point out that in that very same song she also sings, "Can't find my Drinko man."

I'm right here, Gaga. I've always been here.

But anyway, if you want to gamify your life and have a lot more fun, you should take at least one dance break a day. Wouldn't want to let the Gags down.

GAME 28:

THE GO GO PEOPLE

My mom is the original queen of finding the game of life. Anytime we needed to clean our rooms but for sure didn't want to, she would have us play "the Go Go People."

Not only is the name fabulous, the premise is pretty clever. The idea is that we would turn into these super-speedy robot-like people. The Go Go People don't stop and think. They don't take their time. They certainly don't hem and haw. They just clean! Super fast!

I still remember how fun cleaning my room was because of my mom's Go Go People game. I'm not saying this led to the cleanest room possible. (The Go Go People weren't worried about Yelp reviews.) It did, however, lead to finishing the job and having fun in the process.

Just like Dance Break, if you find yourself needing to complete an undesirable task, the Go Go People offers you a way to get the job done while having fun. The spirit is more ripping off the bandage than creating a spreadsheet about how to most efficiently remove it. You following my extended metaphor there?

GAME 29:

GAME DETECTIVE

Take an improv class and you might hear them talking about finding the game in the scene. I'm kind of obsessed with this idea of finding the game.

It just means that as you play make-pretends up there onstage, you're also secretly looking for what's fun in the scene. Maybe a pattern is starting to form. If you're pretending to be in a restaurant ordering a soda and the waiter calls it pop, maybe the game of the scene is to call things by various regional names. If you drop a plate in a scene and your make-pretend brother drops a fork, the game could be dropping anything that belongs on a dinner table.

The game gets really fun when the players push it as far as it can go. In the last example I gave, I don't think I'd be super into the game until people were straight up dropping full Thanksgiving turkeys onto the floor. Ride it until the wheels fall off, as they say.

So your twenty-ninth game is to find the game in your everyday life. Be on the lookout for games that are being created all around you, all the time.

During college, my two besties and I noticed that on a certain brick walkway, people stumbled and sometimes fell. We decided to set up camp on a nearby bench. We proudly proclaimed that "Anyone could fall at any time," as we sat on our bench, ate ice cream, and smoked cigarettes, and waited for innocent passersby to fall on their faces.

More recently, a friend and I were sitting at a café in New York City. We noticed that the café's outdoor seating gave pedestrians a very narrow path to get by, and the sidewalk on this very narrow path was really uneven. Two people in a row tripped on the sidewalk as they passed. Our game was born. That was forever more "our table," and our witty brunch banter was delightfully interspersed with the hilarity of humans tripping.

Okay, I've noticed a pattern with my games. I like when people trip and fall. Does this make me a nice person? No. Do your games have to also revolve around humiliation? Also no. Your games can be nice games. Your games can involve helping people. I'm just asking you to start noticing patterns that are being born all around you, and then play around with those patterns.

Count the number of times your frenemy says the word "like." Drive home using only right turns. Create a scoring system for hitting things with your car. (It's like golf. You don't want a lot of points here.) I don't know what patterns and games you're going to find out there, but I really want you to open your eyes and start looking.

Once, I was back home visiting my dad and his wife and kid. Now, I had been living in the big city for about a decade, so it was easier for me to spot the following, a very country game.

I was sitting in the front yard when the kid ran past me with a rifle, dragging a groundhog carcass behind him. He then said, "Imma see how long it's gonna take the buzzards to get 'im."

He gleefully told the rest of the family about the impending buzzards.

I was a bit taken aback. I'm not gonna lie. But I also saw the game here. Instead of just rolling my eyes and silently judging everyone, I said, "Twenty bucks says the buzzards first touch down in seven minutes."

The whole family was soon betting and speculating. We stared out windows or eagerly waited on the front porch. A totally mundane afternoon turned into a game that we still all talk about, the Buzzard Game.

Go out into the world, brave friends, and find your very own buzzard game.

GAME 30:

DEALER'S CHOICE

Nobody can make up a new game like a child can. Look to them for inspiration as you set out to do just that—and invent game #30 yourself.

I was walking with my then eleven-month-old through our Brooklyn neighborhood when I saw her waving to a passing dog.

"Hi, dog," I said for her.

Then she waved to a house.

So I said, "Hi, house."

This was followed by "Hi, tree" and "Hi, fire hydrant."

A game was born.

The game we had invented was to just say hi to all the things we saw. It was really fun, and a great way for the two of us to connect because we were playing together.

If a less-than-a-year-old baby can invent a game, then so can you.

Think like a baby (meaning, get playful and don't over-think) and invent your own game.

You might clap every time someone else claps or compliment someone in return for every time you're complimented. Ask yourself what your baby-self would do in each moment.

Now, don't get it twisted. I'm not asking you to have a tantrum or poop in your pants. Just use the other nine games in this chapter as inspiration as you set out to invent your own game.

And don't forget to name it. Naming a game somehow makes it better. It gives it heft. Ella and I call our game simply "the Hi Game." You can obviously be more creative when you're creating and naming your own, but, as you've probably noticed, I'm not investing too much time on profound game names.

Hopefully these ten games have helped you see the lighter side of life. There is enough darkness and dreariness in the world. Seeing the joy and silliness can take some practice. But I want you to start flexing that muscle.

It's easy to start taking yourself too seriously. We have responsibilities (unlike babies). We have jobs and people who depend on us to give them food and shelter. We have challenging relationships and prospects that aren't always hopeful. But something that we can also have is joy.

I have seen people in the most dire circumstances find the joy in life. I have seen my mom tell a joke about her breast cancer and heard a man sing "I Got Sunshine" even though he was homeless, jobless, and penniless.

I'm not asking you to ignore the bad things in life or pretend things are better than they are. I'm just asking you to practice also seeing the simple beauty in the mundane, the joyful pattern that can emerge when we start treating life as a game.

LESSON 4

Killing Debbie Downer

(Getting and Staying Positive)

For someone who has improvised half his life, trying to make people laugh beer out their nostrils, I can be the Eeyoriest person in the damn room. Negativity is a tough habit to break, and I want to start out this lesson from a really honest place. It takes constant work and practice to break out of negative thinking, especially if you're starting with your glass half-empty.

Some of you have totally empty glasses with giant cracks down the middle. Some of you don't even have glasses. And the rest threw their glasses against the mantel in a fit of rage.

For all you negative Nancy's out there, there's hope.

Many improv games have positive thinking at their core. Before we can start saying yes and adding onto people's ideas, we have to be generally receptive. This comes from being positive. By positive, I mean seeing the good qualities in people and situations instead of the bad. I don't necessarily even mean optimistic. We aren't worried about what the future holds in improv or in these next ten games. We're just trying to see the inherent good in things.

A caveat: some things are bad. Some things are shitty. I'm not recommending readers put positive spins on alcoholism, abuse, neglect, rape, suicidal ideation, and other truly unthinkable difficulties. These games are not about pretending bad things are good. If you're dealing with something truly difficult like this, I hope you call on your support system, if you have one. Reach out to trained professionals to talk. Go to meetings. Seek help. Take a big step (if you're able, and it's safe for you to do so).

In improv, and in the following ten games, it's not life-or-death things that we're being more positive about. It's our thoughts about other people and their contributions to scenes. In the case of these games, I want you to start thinking more good than bad about the people around you, and what they say and do.

It's easy to say that someone is lazy and that your boss is mean and your car is ugly. It's easy to say that your vacation was boring and that Steve is a loser and the president is an idiot (I don't know who will be president when you're reading this, or if your country even has a president, so no angry emails please).

But I think we get into this negative thinking habit to protect ourselves. It's a defensive wall. It lets us limit our worlds to what feels safe. If I say that I don't like dumb people and lazy people and Los Angeles, I'm trying to excise those things from my world by pushing them away. The problem is, those things aren't going away anytime soon. You can't really protect yourself from difficult people, and you certainly can never shield yourself from the steamy allure of Hollywood. We're probably stuck with these things forever.

Negativity just doesn't work in improvisation. If I'm thinking about how dumb my scene partner's ideas are or how I don't like working with him, I'm sunk. I'll be the one to ruin the scene, not my "bad" scene partner, because I'm the one spending my limited brain space thinking about how bad he is. If I flip my thinking to the positive, I can turn even the worst scene partner into a downright winner. I just have to start seeing the good in what he's saying and doing onstage.

Positivity is scary for some people. It means we're opening up our worlds to the unknown. If I say I hate crowds (and I do say that), I'm trying to stay safe by eliminating them from my life. This might make me safer, but it doesn't make my life richer. By seeing the positive side of crowds—more people to see, more stories to hear, better odds of seeing someone wearing the same shirt as me—I'm adding some chaos and uncertainty back into my life. I'm not just staying at home saying I hate crowds. I'm living my life. Of course, I can't predict how things will unfold now that I'm going with the flow and seeing the good. That can be downright scary! But I think it's the direction that makes life worth living.

Don't spend your life making lists of things you hate. Remove things from the list with each passing day, so that you can experience every possible thing before your ticker stops ticking.

That's what getting and staying positive can do for you. It gets you headed back in the direction of inviting things in as opposed to running away from things. It gets you going with the flow instead of getting out of the lazy river.

And don't we all just want to be in a lazy river?

Okay, I'm out of mixed metaphors. I hope you're at least a little encouraged to start thinking more positively. Here are ten ways you can begin to make it happen.

GAME 31:

AFFIRMATION STATION

Before taking the stage, improvisers aren't thinking about how dumb and unfunny they are. I obviously don't want you starting your day this way either.

A little affirmation can go a long way in switching your mindset from negative to positive. Our thoughts become our reality. At least that's what that *Secret* book Oprah was hawking told me.

Now, I don't believe that if I picture myself driving a fancy-pants red sports car then I'll get one, but I do think that starting the day with positive thoughts allows us to notice more positive things as the day goes on. This means more good things for us, because that's what we have primed ourselves to perceive.

For this game, think about the *Saturday Night Live* sketch "Daily Affirmation with Stuart Smalley" or that YouTube video with the peppy little girl pumping herself up in the mirror. Take a moment to affirm the good in your life. It's best if it's out loud. Just unload the positive. Remind yourself what's good.

You might say how great your husband is for cooking last night, how beautiful the sunset is, how lucky you are for being able to take a vacation in Tahiti, how nice your house is, how loving your dog is, how independent your cat is, or how smart and kind you are.

You can focus on the good things about yourself or the things you're thankful for in your life. Experiment with each type of positive thinking and see which one impacts you more. Do you have better days when you pump yourself up or when you remind yourself about what you're thankful for?

Just be careful not to say a secret sabotage while you're at the Affirmation Station. Don't disguise a negative in positive wording. For example, don't say, "I'm thankful my wife didn't cheat on me again today" or "I love how my kids do whatever they want no matter what I say."

Focusing on what's lacking in our lives is a tough habit to break, so as you practice your affirmations, keep it truly positive.

"I'm happy I get to share my ideas with people in the form of this book" is a much more sincere, positive affirmation than "I'm glad Kanye found Kim. Maybe there's hope for me, too."

You are amazing, and you have a lot of great things going for you. I just want you to start noticing, and then saying that shit out loud. If doing so in front of a mirror helps, go for it. I mean, you know the whole West family is talking to themselves in the mirror. Why can't you?

GAME 32:

THE GOOD BOOK

The next game is to simply start tracking your positive thoughts in writing. Keep a "Good Book." Not the Bible kind, but the kind full of all the good things you can possibly think of.

I like to get my positive thoughts in writing because then I can start to see patterns and where I'm slipping back into subtle negative thinking. It also helps keep me accountable. It's like homework. I have to complete it. Unlike Affirmation Station, where no one can see whether or not I did it.

So grab a composition notebook or a more proper, fancy journal and write down all the good things you can think of. Write down good things about yourself and about your life. What is good about you? What is great about your life? What are you grateful for?

This kind of reflection works best first thing in the morning. It allows you to set the tone for the rest of your day.

You can also end your day with some positive journal writing and see how that starts to improve your days. Be consistent, and keep the writing positive. Don't slip into secret sabotage and don't allow your Good Book to become mundane. I sometimes end up writing to-do lists or what I did that day. But ideally, the Good Book should be more specialized and more sacred. Only positive thinking should go there. Put obsessive, anxious thoughts somewhere else.

Look back at your old entries occasionally. Make sure you're staying positive and not sabotaging with subtle negative thinking. Make sure you aren't just listing secret anxieties.

Looking back can also allow you to notice trends. Do you think a lot about work during the week? Are you only grateful for your wife on Saturdays? Has it been a while since you said anything good about yourself?

Notice, and then try to improve the next time you write in your Good Book. Get more and more positive about more and more things.

I think you'll find that priming yourself to notice good things actually works. It changes our way of thinking to a more receptive, calmer, kinder, happier state.

If I'm thinking about how dumb I am, I'm less likely to think of a solution to a problem at work.

If I'm thinking about how mean my dad is, I'm primed to notice all the bad things about him. I'm looking to prove my theory about his meanness instead of being open to his possible kindness.

Prime yourself in the other direction. Be open to the good in yourself and others, and see if that improves your life.

Think about a rock rolling down a snow-covered hill. If I cover it with snow, it's going to accumulate more snow all the way down. If I cover it with shit, that won't happen.

So at the end of your busy day, do you want a snowman or a shit-rock? Choose carefully.

GAME 33:

DID ANYBODY DIE?

Part of being more positive is keeping things in perspective. It's easy to get trapped in a downward spiral when you let a slightly bad moment be worse than it really is.

When someone rolls their eyes at us, it's easy to start thinking that everything we say is dumb and that they hate us and that they always hated us and that we will most certainly die old and alone.

When your boss asks you to rework your numbers, it can be tempting to start the wicked thought web that she thinks you're incompetent and that she never liked you and that she wants to fire you and that you'll never work in this town again and that you will most certainly die old and alone.

Don't sink into this kind of soap-operatic sludge! Cut off the spiral at the pass.

When you feel a negative thought coming on, practice asking yourself, "Did anybody die?"

The answer is almost always no. And then you have some

instant perspective. Nobody died. The world keeps on spinning.

You broke your favorite wineglass? Nobody died. It's not that bad. You can buy a new one. You shouldn't be drinking so much wine anyway, lady.

You lost your favorite pair of sunglasses? Nobody died. You could buy a new pair. The old ones didn't fit your face. It will be fun to hunt for some new glasses anyway.

One little question can help you reframe your negative thoughts and give you some much needed perspective.

Nobody died, and the world keeps on spinning.

Now, this game probably won't work if someone really did die. If that happened, I'm so sorry. That's awful.

But if you felt negative only when people you loved died, you would be living a pretty positive life.

People become immobilized when they mess up or get fired or say the wrong thing or when someone doesn't like them. It's understandable—I do it myself. But the world keeps on spinning, baby.

And as far as dying old and alone? I can't promise you won't, but that doesn't matter right now! Don't worry about dying old and alone until you're dying old and alone. For right now, did anybody die? No? Okay, then. Keep it moving.

GAME 34:

HIGH FIVES FOR EVERYONE!

There's a lot of high-fiving at improv rehearsals.

There's a lot of high-fiving when I go out to a bar.

High-fiving is like a kinesthetic jump start for positivity. Try high-fiving while frowning. Possible? Yes. But really tough and unnatural feeling.

For this game, you can start by high-fiving people whenever they say or do anything positive. This will give you the added bonus of keeping your positivity radar up and running.

"Thanks for the ride, Mom." Boom. High five!

"Your market report is really solid, Dave." Boom. High five!

"I love your new haircut, June." Boom bam balingo. High fives for everyone!

The simple beauty of a high five is that it connects us through touch. It also disarms us. It's playful and silly. Connect and disarm. High five!

After you've high-fived positive moments, you can try going hog wild. Try high-fiving more promiscuously. High-five sad people and mean people. High-five bank tellers and shop owners. High-five for no discernible reason at all.

I think you'll find that your day gets a little brighter, and you encourage some good vibes from others.

Some people will be put off by your high-fiving. No matter. Take your whimsy elsewhere!

And if global pandemics are harshing your high-fiving vibe, don't you ever forget about virtual high fives.

I wish I could high-five you for even attempting this high-fiving movement, which could sweep the nation if we only let it.

GAME 35:

THE SPIN ROOM

Your old negativity is really just an opportunity for you to practice some newfound positivity.

Improv uses a lot of listing games. There's free association and categories and alphabetical lists. These are all really just warm-ups, methods for getting the brain thinking in a new way, a way that sharpens that dome.

I want you to take all the shitty things about your life, all the things you're negative about, and take them to the metaphorical spin room. You don't need to have a literal room just for this game, but a consistent, private place might help.

Take the list of things you're negative about and practice putting a positive spin on each one.

Let's say your list includes your boss, people who don't wear belts, and your weight. In the spin room you just start putting that positive spin on each.

Your boss is curt because she expects a lot from you. You can learn a lot from her. She is a good dresser and has offered you opportunities you don't focus on enough. Spin.

People who don't wear belts save time at the airport. They don't have to worry about matching it to their shoes. They are smart enough to buy pants that actually fit well. Spin.

Your weight? You look great in that new outfit. Your partner likes the meat on your bones. Some people are starving to death, and you're lucky enough to not have to worry about where your next meal comes from. Spin spin sugar.

The Spin Room is a dedicated time to practice turning our frowns upside down. It's an opportunity to take the things that make us get negative and practice turning them positive.

After the Spin Room, your brain will be primed and ready to be more positive from the get-go. My hope is that this shrinks your negative list, maybe someday keeping you out of the Spin Room altogether. A gal can dream . . .

GAME 36:

ON THE OTHER HAND

Every time you hear yourself get negative, think of it as a chance to practice being more positive.

In one improv game, New Choice, a moderator stops the scene in order to force players to make a new choice. The idea is that the players' third and fourth choices are sometimes much funnier than their first.

For example, a scene might take place at the zoo. It's a father-and-son scene, and they're talking about the father getting back into the dating scene after a divorce. The son might say that his father should start dating. Then, after the moderator says, "New choice," the son might say he needs to take up knitting. Then maybe bowling. Then communing with nature.

The moderator then lets the scene carry on when she is happy with one of the new choices.

This is exactly the kind of new-choicing we should be doing on a daily basis to shift into more positive thinking.

For this game, be on the lookout for negativity spewing out of your mouth. Whenever you catch yourself saying something negative, I want you to weave something positive into that same conversation by adding, "On the other hand . . ."

For example, if you tell someone that your street is always noisy, you can then add, "On the other hand, I'm lucky to live on such a lush, tree-lined street."

If you catch yourself saying, "My wife's cooking isn't what it used to be," you can add, "On the other hand, she is still my most trusted sounding board and friend." This added positivity might also make you realize that it's the twenty-first century and you should probably be doing half the cooking yourself anyway.

Give yourself a point for every "On the other hand" you pull off successfully. See how adding something positive changes how you start to view things. And if it doesn't, hey, at least you got some points.

See what I did there?

GAME 37:

ONE STEP BACK,
TWO STEPS FORWARD

Now it's time to take the training wheels off. This time, when you catch yourself saying something negative, you have to weave in two positive things. You don't have to say, "On the other hand," but you can if it still helps.

Aim for honest, sincere positive statements.

Every time you slip up and sink into negativity, see it as an opportunity to say double the positives.

And I'll let you have two points each time you correct yourself with two positive statements.

What do you do with these points?

I don't know. They don't really mean anything. But some people like points.

GAME 38:

JUST KIDDING . . . IT'S GOOD!

I want to give you one more way to get yourself out of your negative rants.

It may not be the most sophisticated way to turn the tides of negativity, but each time you hear yourself going negative, simply say, "Just kidding."

I like this approach because it adds some levity to your positivity quest.

"I hate my neighbors."

"Just kidding. They're not that bad."

"I look like crap."

"Just kidding. I've still got it."

"My kids are annoying."

"Just kidding. I love them more than anything."

This game is like an emergency break. You're not weaving positivity in as much as stopping the negativity dead in its tracks.

This game will help you notice when you're getting negative, and noticing is half the battle. You may be surprised at how often it is. Use the last three games to try to pull it back. How do people react? How does it make you feel to flip to more positive statements? How does it affect your conversations?

Now that you're a master at the self-correct, let's see if you can also help other people get out of their murky negative no-nos.

GAME 39:

PLUS POSITIVE

Improv is all about adding onto what someone else contributes to a scene. If someone says they have a dog, you can add that you like his pretty black fur. You could also add that you're allergic to dogs. This happens a lot with novice improvisers. No matter what someone says, they add something salty.

Don't be like them.

Now is your chance to add something sweet.

For this game, you will be adding positive comments to what others say and even turning their negative comments positive.

Anything is possible.

In improv, when someone makes a statement, we call it an initiation. I want you to add onto other people's initiations with positive statements.

If someone says they got a promotion, you can say they deserve it because they work so hard.

Don't say that you also got a promotion or okay or that you don't care.

If someone says they cleaned their room, you can say they're so motivated and on top of their life.

Don't say what or why or that you cleaned your whole house.

If someone says they're going on vacation, you can say you still remember the pictures from their last beautiful trip to Copenhagen.

Don't say you just got back from vacation or you never get to take vacations.

There is a difference between adding something positive to the conversation and just keeping the conversation going. You want to add something truly positive. Don't talk about yourself. Don't ask questions. Don't compare. Don't judge.

Just add something positive.

Then if you truly master that, try to turn even negative remarks in a positive direction.

If someone says their back hurts, you can say that you've noticed how hard they've been working.

Don't tell them it's not that bad or that they should've gone to the doctor a month ago like you told them.

If someone says they hate their job, you can say that she's added so much to that company and that she's so good at what she does.

Don't say that a person shouldn't hate her job or that it's not that bad.

If someone says that Kim Kardashian doesn't deserve to be famous, then you're on your own. I'm sure there's some way to put a positive spin on this line of thinking.

Be very careful not to invalidate people's feelings. You aren't disagreeing with their negative view. You are just weaving something positive in. Don't tell people how to feel. Just try keeping things positive.

To prove how amazing this game is, I'll give the Kim Kardashian example a try. You could say that Kim Kardashian . . . okay, this is tough for me . . . knows what products to use for her hair, or that you actually like her interior design choices.

I feel more positive and happy already.

Get out there and make positive contributions to conversations.

Don't tell people not to be negative. Don't tell people to be positive.

Just do what your parents always droned on about: say something nice.

GAME 40:

THE YAY GAME

It's finally time for me to tell you about my absolute favorite improv game. I call it the Yay Game, but I'm sure it goes by many other names and can be played many other ways.[1]

In the version I'm familiar with, everyone stands in a circle and marches because they're about to go on a make-pretend adventure, and I just feel like the marching helps everyone get more into it. Then one person volunteers the first line of an adventure, maybe "We're going into outer space!" It's important that the phrase starts with "We" and that it ends with an exclamation point. It's an adventure, not a trip to the corner store.

Then everyone has to lift both arms high and yell, "Yay!" Again, we're talking big excitement exclamation marks here.

Then someone else adds to the adventure. If they were going into outer space, maybe the next line could be "We fly past a satellite!" And then another "Yay!" And on and on.

Inevitably someone will volunteer something not-so-fun, like "We die!" or "Our liver gets cirrhosis!" Obviously, no one wants to yay that shit. But the Yay Game demands it. So pretend the guy who said that isn't an asshat and just say "Yay!"

People say things on the regular that we don't want to yay. Here's where the Yay Game comes in for you.

I want you to make your everyday life much more of an adventure by yaying. Get to work on time? Yay!

Drive the speed limit? Yay!

Order a salad for lunch? Yay!

I want you to literally say "Yay!" at these mundane everyday occurrences.

And once you master yaying some good things throughout your day, I want you to start yaying not-so-good things.

Get to work late? Yay! At least you got there!

Drive fifteen over the speed limit and get a ticket? Yay! You didn't die!

Order a McGriddles and vanilla cone for lunch? Yay! That shit tastes good!

Don't let negative occurrences stay negative. Don't let the asshat win. Just yay that shit and see how it makes you feel.

Congratulations! And yay! You have played forty games so far. I hope you're feeling more grounded, fun, and positive. I hope you're starting to walk out your door with a more playful spirit every morning.

Now it's time to turn our attention to how judgmental you can be. If I'm being self-aware here, I will tell you that I can sometimes be the leader of the asshats, with enough cattiness and pettiness for a thousand lifetimes. So let's start playing our way less judgy.

TIME-OUT:
LET'S TALK ABOUT YOUR PHONE

I'm going to be asking you to mix and mingle with people in ways that you might find slightly—or more than slightly—uncomfortable.

Many of you may feel the need to fall back on some crutches. Not like the kind that help you walk, but the kind that help you disengage with the people around you.

Smartphones are the first thing that comes to mind. When I don't want to interact with people, I get out my phone. I pretend I need to check text messages or Facebook for the fiftieth time that day. If your phone is a way for you to disengage, I want you to find ways to limit your screen time.

You can have a lockbox for your phone, at home or in the car. Place your phone in the box so you won't be tempted to check it all the time. You can also have designated times when you don't use your phone, like at meals.

Definitely challenge yourself, while you play these games, to not just use your phone as a way to disengage.

And aim to be as present in your real-life scenes as humanly possible.

Now put down the phone and proceed.

LESSON 5

Thou Shalt Not
Be Judgy

O f the many unhelpful thoughts running through my head, the most toxic may be my judginess. When I think that someone is too slow, too dumb, or too ugly, I'm missing out on the tons of good things they actually are. Even when I think someone is too aggressive, too pretentious, or too ruggedly good-looking, I'm still not seeing the reality of my present situation.

I'm not in the moment, and arguably, I'm also kind of a jerk.

Judgment is a way we protect ourselves. If I write someone off, I don't have to slog through a genuine interaction with them. I don't have to get to know them.

Snap judgment saves me from rejection. I write people off before they can do the same to me.

Unfortunately, like many self-defense mechanisms, judgment often has the opposite effect. I mean, who wants to hang out with the judgy lady?

Being judgmental repels people. If you aren't open to new interactions, they start to happen less often.

In improv, judgment is a way to pre-script a scene. It's a way to say no, and it's a real scene-ender. For improv to work, I have to think the best of my teammates and be open to every contribution they bring to our scenes. Judgment gets in the way of this.

Imagine you're in a scene with someone. Before you even walk on the stage, you roll your eyes. This improviser is so annoying!

Here you are, thinking about things you don't like about your partner, while you could have been noticing the funny way they walked onto the stage. You also missed the name they imbued you with. Your partner called you "Debbie," and in ten seconds you're going to introduce yourself as "Fred" because you were judging and not listening. In short, you missed out because you weren't in the moment with your partner.

The same thing happens IRL (or "in real life" as the kids say). I can't be thinking about snap judgments or I'll miss out on what's unfolding right in front of me.

So knock it off. I know it's easier said than done. Judging people is a nasty habit that's hard to shake.

Luckily for you, here are ten games that will help you stop judging and start seeing what's really going on.

GAME 41:

I GOT YOUR BACK

It's a fairly common improv tradition to pat each and every one of your teammates on the back while saying, "I got your back" before taking the stage. More than a few times, I thought about how great it would be if my family, friends, and coworkers reminded me that they were on my side, that they wanted me to be awesome.

So be the change you want to see in the world. Tell people that you have their back or that you're on their side or that you want them to succeed or be exceptional.

During an improv show, it behooves you to make your teammates look good. The better they are, the better you look. I think the real world works the same way. Belittling someone doesn't make you look good. It doesn't make the office run more smoothly. It doesn't keep your marriage plodding along.

Making others look good makes us look good.

So literally tell people that you've "got their back." Tell people that you're rooting for them.

You can even make a tradition out of it. Before an important meeting, walk around and tell each of your coworkers that you got their back.

Before dinner, toast every family member and say it. "I got your back!"

Negative thoughts quickly get stuck on a loop in my head.

I'm quick to assume the worst and to get defensive. Saying that I have people's backs and hearing that they have mine is the warp zone I need to stop that infernal judgment.

So provide this supportive environment wherever you go.

Tell people you have their backs—then make sure you do.

GAME 42:

TRY SOMETHING ELSE (NOT JUDGY)

Yes, we're back to the New Choice–inspired genre. Instead of just making a new choice when you're negative, now I want you to make a new choice when you judge someone.

After tracking my own judgementality for a few hours, I got some terrible examples straight from my dome. I want you to know what kind of judgmental thoughts you're looking for. Plus, I have little to no shame in my game.

"Idiot," "slowpoke," "unhappy," "bad dresser," "jerk," "pretentious," "lazy," and "didn't get hugged enough as a child."

By thinking this way, I'm missing out on people's actual intelligence, kindness, and love. I don't want to miss out anymore! And I don't want you to either.

So next time your brain gets judgmental and makes snap judgments about others, I want you to stop. Really, I want you to pause. Take a time-out. Then I want you to try something else.

Instead of assuming they're an idiot, find out their eye color.

Instead of writing them off as a jerk, try to see what they're doing or who they're with.

Make a nonjudgmental observation about that person. Learn more about them.

They may actually be an idiot or a jerk, but I want you to slow your roll and learn more about them before settling on these harsh judgments.

After all, there are some nice idiots and some funny jerks out there. Be the change . . .

GAME 43:

JUST ASK

As a natural extension of Try Something Else (Not Judgy), this game simply asks you to ask them. When you interact with someone, old or new, ask at least three questions.

Ask where they get their hair done, where they're from, where they live, or where they bought that shirt.

Ask if they have siblings, if they went to college, or what their favorite dance move is.

Ask them their favorite moment from today, or what makes them laugh.

Then listen to them when they answer!

GAME 44:

CURIOUS DETECTIVE

Curious Detective takes the last game and steps it up a few notches. Imagine you're Columbo. If you don't remember Columbo, good on you. That means you're younger than I am, and I refuse to be judgmental about the fact that you were born in the 1990s or 2000s.

Columbo was this gumshoe-type TV detective, real sleuthy. He would poke his nose around and gather clues and solve the case.

You could also be Sherlock Holmes, or a junior investigator looking for Carmen Sandiego, if that's your flavor. The point is, you're a detective.

Now, you're not trying to solve a crime. You're just trying to crack the case of who the person you're talking to really is. What makes them tick?

Get to the bottom of what makes them special and what their values are.

Ask questions, observe body language, and listen carefully to every response.

This will help you to stop thinking about yourself and stop judging others.

True curiosity about others helps to engage us more fully during interactions (and learn more about the world).

So put on your detective hat and actually give a shit the next time you chat someone up.

GAME 45:

HOW DO YOU KNOW?

I think some of these games must come from having the voice of my mother splashing around my gray matter for four decades. But let's go with it. Sometimes Mother really does know best.

The next time you catch yourself getting judgy with it, I want you to ask yourself, "How do you know?"

It's a simple question, and it sounds a lot like something your parents might say when they overhear you being judgmental.

"How do you know?"

How do you know she's dumb? How do you know he will be mean? How do you know that person is going to be dull?

Nine times out of ten (not an actual statistic!) the answer will be, you don't.

If your answer is that you just know, then you know you can do better!

I think asking the question—and struggling to answer—is a worthwhile exercise.

Because the answer 91 percent of the time (truly, I'm just making up numbers) is that you really don't know.

And when you don't know, get to know.

Right, Mom?

GAME 46:

IF YOU CAN'T
SAY ANYTHING NICE . . .

Here's another one straight from the mom playbook. If you can't say something nice, don't say anything at all.

It's easy to forget about this simple rule. But it's an oldie and a goodie.

When you catch yourself shit-talking someone behind their back, just stop. It's better to sit in silence than to keep being harsh and judgmental.

Silently sip your drink.

Silently watch TV.

Silently just be silent!

Anything is better than the rude negativity that's ready to spew forth from your meany face.

Talk about the weather.

Talk about that local sports team.

Talk about how you can't think of what to talk about.

Anything is better than being judgmental.

And enjoy the silence.

Filling every moment with chatter is an easy habit to get into. Break the habit. Stop judging, and just be . . .

. . . quiet.

GAME 47:

THE WAVE GAME

You learn some games from your mom. You learn others from your infant daughter. This is the lesson on not judging, so don't judge me.

As I pushed baby Ella in her stroller, I noticed that she waved to every single person we passed on the street. It was this precious Queen Elizabeth II kind of a wave, very regal yet sincere. I'm raising her right. She's not above it all.

But truly, she was feeling this waving.

I want that for us. I know some of you live in areas where people wave to each other on the regular already. This won't be so weird for you.

On the other hand, some of you live in places where waving to everyone you pass is impractical or might not end well.

Let's keep safety front and center as we decide who we will wave to and who we won't.

The aim here, though, is to greet people warmly. Many improv classes start with players circulating the room and high-fiving or shaking hands and patting each other on the back. Bring this playful warmth into your everyday life.

Maybe you decide it's only safe to greet people at your office, and not on your block. Fine. It's a great place to start.

Say "Good morning" and wave when you see them in the parking lot.

Maybe you feel okay about waving at the people in your neighborhood, whether you know them or not. Also fine. See what happens when you wave. I bet more people will greet you. I also bet you will just feel happier.

Waving isn't as magical as a high five, in my opinion, but it still gives you all those warm feelings of connection.

Whether you're trying the Wave Game at home or at work, I want to encourage you, barring safety concerns, not to pick and choose who you will wave at. That's judgment!

Think you have a cold boss? Wave at her anyway! Your judgment might be why she's cold in the first place. It may be a self-fulfilling prophecy.

We have loads of unconscious and conscious biases. So once you pick your waving hot spot, let her rip. Wave at every and all without a single ounce of judgment or bias.

And see what happens next. Just like high-fiving, I think you're gonna really like it.

I wish there was a way for me to wave at you right now.

(I just waved at my computer screen.)

Did you feel the love?

GAME 48:

STRANGER NOT DANGER

Repeat after me, "A stranger is just a friend I haven't met yet."

That's got to be the new mantra.

Too many times, I'm overwhelmed with negative thoughts when I meet new people.

They won't like me. They don't care what I'm saying. They're bored. I sound stupid.

Look what I've done. I've turned this new person into a monster.

It's just not fair for me to do that.

So say it again, "A stranger is just a friend I haven't met yet."

You don't know this person. Start with a clean slate. They might be your new best friend, your future spouse, or your long-lost sister who had amnesia.

You're never gonna find out if you have already turned yourself into a dumb dumb and them into a meany face.

This new person is nothing but potential greatness.

"A stranger is just a friend I haven't met yet."

Now go!

GAME 49:

ENERGY MATCH

Part of improv's brilliance is its simplicity. It's totally scary to jump onstage and have no earthly idea what's going to happen next. You don't know what character you will play or even what the setting is going to be. It's a little like jumping out of a plane . . . without a parachute.

But you have a net. And that net is to just do what your teammates are doing. Match them somehow.

Energy matching is when I try to be at the same energy level as my scene partner. If they're frantic and pacing, I step up my energy level.

I'm not copying them. I don't have to have the same frantic quality. But we both should be high-energy.

Same goes for low-energy, and everything in between.

I love energy matching because it gets me out of my own head. I have to really focus on my scene partner to make sure I'm on the same page.

It also stops me from judging what my partner is doing. If I have to match them, I'm not judging that choice. I'm embracing and mirroring that choice.

I'm joining the fun.

I want you to try this in your everyday interactions. Try to match the energy level of the people you interact with. It helps me to rate their energy level on a scale from one to ten. In your head, start identifying who is giving you a one-energy (think Eeyore) and who is giving you a ten (think Tigger).

Then match it.

If Bill in Sales had too much coffee, I want you to ramp it up. Move more. Nod in agreement. Animate your face more.

If your mother-in-law is jet-lagged from the long flight, tone it down. Slow down that breathing. Relax and lower your voice.

It is essential that this not become a game of copycat. Just like when you played that game when you were five, it's still annoying as hell.

You aren't making fun or mimicking. You are just trying to match people's general energy level. Make it subtle. Make trying not to get caught part of the game.

And whatever you do, do not blame me if you piss off your mother-in-law.

GAME 50:

STATUS MATCH

Another matching game is called status matching. Keith Johnstone is the go-to guy for all things status related.[1] His theory, if I can oversimplify the hell out of it, is that we're animals, and animals are all about the pecking order. We are always negotiating our own place in the pecking order based on the behaviors of others.

The example I always use is when you're walking down the street and someone is coming toward you in the opposite direction. If you're both fighting for the same status, the result is that side-to-side shuffle where both people struggle to pass by each other.

If someone is stomping down the street in a power suit and a briefcase, I usually lower my status and let them pass.

If I'm stomping down the street with my sunglasses and a business suit (this rarely happens!), I'm not about to get out of anyone's way. I'm really feeling myself and my high status, so some shoulders might be getting bumped.

The point here is that all of us are already negotiating our status based on other people, and we can use this insight in our everyday lives. So start paying attention to other people's status.

Give it a number. Give me a ten when I'm stompin' with my sunglasses and suit.

Give that mousy person a one when they avoid eye contact and keep their eyes pointed to the sidewalk.

Then match people's status.

If your friend Karen is averting her eyes and has her feet angled in, don't puff out your chest and speak louder. Instead, droop your shoulders and lower your voice.

Try this while you're walking down the street, too. Try to be at the average status of everyone around you. This is a different game on Wall Street than it is in Woodstock.

The point here is not to judge people's status: "She's pathetic" or "He's a jerk."

The point is to try it out, to walk in their shoes . . . or at least walk in their status.

We tend to be much less judgmental when we try to embody someone else's experience. So get ready to notice people's status and not their faults. Get ready to try out their status instead of overthinking all the things you don't like about them.

I think you'll get the added benefit of learning more about yourself in the process.

Now, it's one thing to try to not judge others, to decrease those snap judgments. It's another to think the world of every single person you meet.

Everyone is a genius.

If that's a tough idea to swallow, we have some play to do. So let's get started.

LESSON 6
World of Geniuses

Now that you've accepted that not everyone is a dumb jerk, it's time to turn up the heat. Now you need to embrace the improv principle that we must treat each other as if we're all geniuses, poets, and artists.

Del Close, a pioneer in the improv world, once said that if we treat each other as if we're geniuses, poets, and artists, we have a better chance of becoming that onstage.[1]

What if that were true in real life, too? What if we needed to treat each other like winners in order to really win at this game called life?

It makes sense, doesn't it? If you treat your employees like dumb dumbs, they won't rise to the occasion. They won't stay late, work as hard as they can for you, or have the confidence to innovate.

If you treat your family like losers, they'll be more likely to lose.

I guess it's as simple as what goes around comes around. Self-fulfilling prophecies and all that.

When we treat others with absolute reverence, we are more revered.

So dig deep and take a few slow and steady breaths. It's time to start treating others like they're the pot of gold at the end of the rainbow. People are miracles made of magic. You're just late to the party. Try to keep up.

GAME 51:

COMPLIMENT STEW

We don't compliment each other enough. Most people go through their day without hearing many compliments, and they certainly aren't giving enough of them away.

Compliments aren't retirement plans. You don't have to hoard them or save them all up, so you can retire in Belize with your lover. Seriously, they don't work that way at all.

Compliments should be given freely. I want you to be a compliment whore. Just give them out like it's going out of style.

Didn't Dolly Levi say that money is like manure? It's only good when it's spread around? Well, compliments are the new manure!

So start spreading those compliments!

Compliment people for their clothes, their kindness, their

contributions, and their décor. Compliment people's hard work, their preparation, their friendship, and their cooking.

Compliment freely. But honesty is crucial here. Like a Great White can smell a drop of blood from a mile away, people can smell a phony compliment.

I want you to compliment every single person you talk to at least once per interaction, a one-for-one. Talk to one person one time? You're giving 'em one compliment. Easy peasy.

Talk to two people two different times? That's four compliments! Two compliments per person. I hope you're starting to get this. Math is hard.

Then I want you to note what happens when you start this Compliment Stew. Record it in your journal if you're still keeping that old thing going.

Complimenting people will brighten their days, and it will start to open your eyes to all the ways they're fantastic, a good first step toward seeing them as geniuses, poets, and artists.

GAME 52:

IMBUE WITH GREATNESS

One way to start seeing people's greatness is to just visualize it. Just do it, as Nike would say.

In improv, you can imbue others with whatever qualities you like. You can make someone a carrot, a pheasant, or a Dorito. You could also imbue them with the traits of a genius, poet, or artist. Or Pitbull. You could imbue them with the qualities of Pitbull.

The point here is that we have the power to visualize others' greatness.

The next time you're small-talking, I want you to imbue the person you're talking to with absolute greatness. Picture them as special, as sacred, as someone who truly matters and makes a difference. Notice how their hands look like they work hard, and their crow's-feet show the warmth of their spirit. Get deep with it. Pretend you're the Dalai Lama if you have to.

But whatever you do, visualize greatness.

For one, the more you're focused on them, the less you're focused on yourself. That's an immediate win.

For B, filling up your head with the greatness of your talk buddy will help you start to walk the walk. You'll start to see the greatness if you're looking for it.

Make someone great, and they'll be great. Our expectations for others affect their behavior, so this simple exercise of imbuing with greatness should help them step up to the plate and actually be great.

If nothing else, this game gives you a chance to take a break from the negative pinwheel of your mind. It never hurts to have more positive thoughts bubbling around up there.

GAME 53:

POETRY TO MY EARS

Now it's time to start hearing other people's words as the poetry they are.

I'm not talking Dr. Seuss here.

For this game, I want you to put on your imaginary—or literal, why not?—beret and snap those fingers. Smoke that imaginary cigarette with the fancy cigarette holder in the smoky jazz lounge. And listen for the poetry in the mundane.

When you're talking with someone, I want you to listen for the poetry hidden in their everyday words. Rhythm and repetition are smuggled in our everyday speech. Shakespeare's iambic pentameter (duh DUH duh DUH duh DUH duh DUH duh DUH) comes from how we naturally speak anyway. Shakespeare knew there was natural poetry in our everyday speech. It's time for you to learn the same lesson. And just like that, sha blam, you're Shakespeare.

So . . . when you're talking with someone, listen for something poetic in what they say. It could be how they repeat a sound or a word or a phrase. It could be the rhythm of their words or how they pause between thoughts.

Notice the poetry and then repeat it. Out loud. Without comment. Just repeat the part that you found poetic. They might ask why you're repeating them. If they do, just say that it was good or that you liked how they said that. Then you're back playing Compliment Stew.

Look at you! You are a game-playing wizard at this point. Keep up the good work.

GAME 54:

YOU ARE A UNICORN SLIDING DOWN A RAINBOW

I get stuck in the habit of dehumanizing hordes of people. Walking down the streets of a big city, it's easy for me to stop thinking of the sea of people as people. I'm not thinking of them as walruses or emus either. I'm just thinking of them as a mass—a soulless, mindless clump.

That's the habit we have to break. Each one of those people out there is just that—a person.

Whether you're at a board meeting, the dinner table, or waiting in line to buy a designer, slow-drip babyccino, I want you to break the habit of thinking of people as a group.

I want you to search their souls for what makes them magic, sparkling unicorns.

At a board meeting? Instead of waiting for the Cleveland office to join the conference call while checking your Facebook, take a moment to look at each and every person around that table. As you look at each person, think of one thing that makes him or her a miracle among miracles, a gold star, a ten.

Waiting for Dad to serve up tonight's dinner? Give each person a moment's eye contact and a special thought. Dad is tall. Mom is funny. Sister is a good singer. Brother is open-hearted. Congratulations! Your family is freakin' sweet AF.

Waiting in line for that coffee? Find the sparkle for each and every other person in line and everyone who works there. Even places that serve babyccinos are staffed with miracles and unicorns.

Now, what happens when people do not seem like miracles? This is real life, after all. Sometimes people are bullies and jerks and meanies.

Just think of this as an added challenge.

What makes that bully, jerk, or meany freakin' awesome?

The harder it is to find, the better you'll be at this game . . . and therefore life.

So find the magic. Find the rainbow. Ride the unicorn.

GAME 55:

TEACH ME, SENSEI

No one likes a know-it-all. And I'm pretty sure Socrates said something about wisdom being all about knowing how you don't know anything. I'm paraphrasing, obvi.

People enjoy a lifelong learner, someone who is open to new ideas. If you have a lot of money and you think you can't learn anything from poor people, your perspective got all messed up somewhere along the way.

If you're a boomer who thinks they can't learn from a millennial, your clothes aren't the only thing out of date.

If you're a Democrat who thinks they can't learn anything from a Republican, your reality got hijacked in all the infotainment out there.

We can all learn from everyone else! That's what I'm trying to say here.

So listen carefully. Take notes if you have to. Constantly listen for nuggets of wisdom no matter who you're talking to.

If I can learn from my toddler, you can learn from your boss.

If I can learn from my students, you can learn from your wife.

Let's go back to my Kim Kardashian example. What can I learn from her?

There's something about her hazy, baby voice I can learn from. I don't have to always be on and alert. Sometimes sounding like you're in a chill haze can make you seem famous and powerful. I should relax more and let them come to me.

How'd I do? Does that count?

But on the real, Kim K is allegedly studying to be a lawyer because of her strongly held belief that our judicial system is broken. There's actually a ton to learn from her commitment, conviction, and ability to work across party lines and redefine herself in service of a cause. You just have to give it a minute and focus on the positive and the possibilities, not the hazy baby voice.

Now you give it a try.

Back to school time. Get out there and learn from every single person you encounter.

GAME 56:

PET PEEVE? PET PRO!

I made this game up while my dog was hacking things up in the living room.

Stay with me. It's a good one.

So my dog is retching like he always does. I take him to the vet. They say he's fine. I guess tiny dogs have tiny throats and a host of medical problems as a result of inhumane inbreeding.

But I digress. My dog Tanzen was hacking. In that moment, I had a choice. I chose to be annoyed. I said, "All day! You do this all day! You're so annoying."

Now, none of these things are lies. He does hack all day, and it is annoying. But I can do better than this. I have another choice.

I can turn my annoyance, my pet peeve, into a positive, a pet pro. And it's kind of a pun because Tanzen is my pet. I'm not great at puns, but I feel like I kind of nailed that one.

I can choose to see Tanzen's hacking as the thing that makes him a superstar. Do all dogs hack? No. Does mine? Yes! See, he's special. My dog is amazing because he hacks.

This takes constant practice because I truly am annoyed at his hacking, but if I dwell on how it annoys me, it will continue to annoy.

So practice the other choice. Choose one annoying thing that one person does and flip that shit to a pet pro.

Man cutting his nails on the train? Pet pro . . . he is concerned about his nail health! Good for him!

Woman chewing with her mouth open? Pet pro . . . there's a rhythm to that chewing that reminds you of a Rihanna song!

Husband forget to take out the trash again? Pet pro . . . he's saving his energy for later . . . in the bedroom . . . bow chicka bow wow!

I don't know what kind of mental gymnastics you're going to have to do, but I think it's going to be good for you to confront your pet peeves.

And make the other choice. Don't give people the power to annoy you.

Turn their annoying habits into what makes them fabulous.

And the less annoyed you are at others, the more leeway they're likely to give you.

Because . . . spoiler alert: you're also super annoying.

Sorry, not sorry.

GAME 57:

THE PAPARAZZO GAME

If we're being honest, and by now I think you know that I am, I'll tell you that I used to pretend I was famous. I think a lot of people do this. They put on ridiculous sunglasses, grab a coffee, and prance down the street pretending they really are someone.

I think this is fine. Fake it till you make it and all.

But that's not this game, because this game isn't about you.

Thinking about yourself doesn't help you interact better with people, so stop thinking you're famous and start pretending everyone else is.

For passersby, I want you to imagine they're all famous rock stars or country singers or YA authors or talk show hosts. Really try to imagine it.

Then see how that affects how you feel about those crowds.

And when you're actually talking with someone, I want you to imagine it's a meet and greet. This person is famous and busy and important, and they're talking to you!

Note how this affects your conversations.

Are you listening more? Are you giving people the benefit of the doubt? Are you thinking more positively about others?

You might want to make a list of all the different types of celebrities before you start.

This way, you won't make everyone a Kardashian.

Don't make everyone a Kardashian.

GAME 58:

FIND THE SUPERHERO

Think about how differently people treat Clark Kent compared to how they treat Superman. Totally unfair, right? It's the same person!

I don't want you to ever make that mistake again, friend. From now on, I want you to muster all your powers of observation so you can identify every person's superhero self.

Waiting in line at the fair? That man in front of you has a flannel shirt and a plaid patch on his jeans. He is Super Farmer or Super '90s Alt Rock Fan or even Super Scottish Man.

Sure, you don't know this guy, so you can't really use his actual strengths, but even a superficial superhero is better than "Man Who Cut the Line and I Want to Punch."

We're going for positivity here, as always.

If you know someone, it's even better. Identify Super Friend and Super Listener and Super Baker and Super Comedian in your life.

If you're getting to know someone, it's the best. This game will remind you to be on the lookout for someone's super-strength.

And just like Clark Kent doesn't have to reveal his super-hero identity, there's no need for you to tell people theirs.

Unless you wanna.

GAME 59:

SELFLESS SELFIES

I may not be a millennial, but I know what they're into.

Selfies.

See? I'm hip.

Now, if you truly want to make someone feel like a genius, poet, or artist . . . or reality TV or YouTube star, you just have to pose for a selfie with them.

It's just that easy. This works especially well with millennials, but I like to think anyone would be flattered at the invitation to join a selfie.

Can you delete said selfie immediately after taking it? Well, yeah, as long as they're not still around.

The prize here is in the selfie taking. It's in the invitation to selfie.

So make people feel spectacular. Get out your phone and ask them to join the shot.

GAME 60:

SINCERE SMILES

Research has shown that smiling makes you happier.[2]

And I think we all know that when you smile the whole world smiles with you.

We're ending this lesson with a simple game. In order to help you treat people like geniuses, poets, and artists, I want you to smile at them.

Start with a smile before you speak.

Look directly into their eyes, smile, and then you may speak.

Smile at the cashier.

Smile at the car driving by.

Smile at your hacking dog.

Smile at your yoga instructor.

Smile at your husband.

It's important to get in the habit of leading with a smile.

Husband walks through the door? Smile first.

Baby wakes up crying? Walk into that room with a sympathetic smile on your mug.

Boss calls you into her office? Smile. It's nice to get to talk with your boss.

Now, I'm not suggesting you smile for the rest of your life no matter what. You definitely shouldn't smile when some jerk says you'd look prettier if only you'd smile. Gross. But for the purposes of this game, try sincerely smiling for a day. Treat every person you encounter today with the utmost care and concern. If everyone is a genius, poet, and artist, the least you can do is start interactions on the right foot, with a smile. Try it out and see what happens. See how it feels. And see how smiling affects your encounters with other people.

Now that we've practiced judging people less and revering

them more, it's time for a lesson I would have thought all but impossible in my twenties.

It's time to face the difficult fact that you are 100 percent not special. You are exactly equal in specialness to every other human the world over.

It's a tough pill for some to swallow. I'll give you a page turn to begin to digest it.

LESSON 7

Your Mom Was Wrong

(You Aren't Special)

Now, this lesson is going to seem to go against what many people are brought up to think. I know I was told over and over how special I was.

I mean, turn on most kids' shows, and they're constantly talking about how special each and every one of us is.

Unfortunately, this message isn't as clear as I think it should be. In reality, we're all equally special. No one is more or less special than anyone else.

Exceptionalism is a great way to turn your kid into an ass-hat. Yes, we all have strengths, but no one is better than anyone else.

Another way to say the same thing is that no one is special. If we're all equally great, then no one is great. There's no ranking, no list, no winner.

It feels sacrilegious to even be typing this, but you're not special!

You are a part, just one tiny part, of something much bigger and more powerful than an individual special you.

You are one of many in your family, community, and world. Your needs are no more or less important than anyone else's.

So stop thinking that you're special, that you're more important, or that your contributions are more valuable than anyone else's.

Instead, take a lesson from our ant friends. They all just perform their role. Ants don't think about their individual exceptionalism. They simply act for the good of the group.

The complexity of the ant society, why humans feel compelled to keep ant houses, is a result of the group interactivity.[1] An ant, on her own, is a failure. Her heroic journey for food may never result in her finding anything. If she didn't have her ant peeps, she might die in vain.

But because millions of ants are all on this same heroic journey, inevitably one of them finds food. She stays there. Another ant stumbles upon the food and then another and another. Now there are a few little ant trails leading somewhere. Soon thousands of ants are streaming toward this food source. The group is what matters and what creates greatness and complexity.

I think humans are at their best when we think more like ants. We aren't special. We are just on a heroic ant journey looking for food . . . or contentment . . . or money . . . or happiness . . . or love.

But sometimes we don't find it. If we don't give up our exceptionalism and defer to the good of the group, we may die in vain.

So let's practice thinking of ourselves as one among many.

And stop thinking of the world revolving around our own axis.

That's too much pressure on you, and it isolates you from everyone else . . . who is equally as lovely and special as you are.

For simplicity's sake, once again, you are not, and never have been, special.

Got it?

GAME 61:

MIRROR MIRROR

You may have been under the impression that you were more special than the people around you. Your parents might still tell you just how special you are even though you still live on their sofa and don't have a job yet and also you're fifty-six years old.

So let's start this despecializing journey before it's too late.

I want you to start to see yourself with more of a blank slate. No rose-colored glasses, but also no harsh criticisms. Just a person.

This is a literal mirror exercise. You're going to stand in front of a mirror. Stand neutrally with your arms to your sides and your feet shoulder-width apart.

I want you to move every time your reflection moves. You are going to mirror your reflection.

If you see your hand wiggle, wiggle your hand in the exact same way. Try not to have a delay. With a mirror exercise, you're trying to mirror at the exact same time. You know . . . like a mirror.

If you see your cheeks start to smile, smile at the exact same time as your reflection.

As you mirror your mirror, I want you to try to gently let any thoughts about how good or bad you are float away. You aren't looking in the mirror to inspect your so-called fat thighs. You're also not looking in the mirror to admire your beautiful new hairdo.

Try to slow your breathing and follow your own simple, subtle movements. It should kind of feel like a meditation.

This mirroring is an important step in being able to move through some later improv-inspired games. If you can't mirror yourself, you won't be able to mirror others.

So take a deep breath and do what you do. Literally.

GAME 62:

THE MIRROR GAME

A classic Viola Spolin improv exercise is the mirror exercise.[2] Two people face each other. In one version, one person is the leader and the other tries to mirror them. Then they switch.

The other version is where I want to focus. In this version, no one is the leader. Spolin calls this exercise Follow the Follower,[3] which I think sums it up beautifully. Everyone is a follower. No leaders here.

Both players stand neutrally facing each other, arms to their sides, feet shoulder-width apart. Each person pays attention to the slight, natural movements of the other. No one is making a move for the other to follow, but moves happen anyway. It's impossible to not move at all. I mean, we have to breathe and stuff.

Then each partner should perceive these subtle movements in the other and duplicate them exactly, no exaggerating. The partners should aim to move at the same time. It shouldn't feel like anyone is leading.

I want you to take this classic mirror exercise to the streets. People spend a lot of time thinking about themselves as separate, of others as obstacles or challenges. In order to start getting more in sync with the hum of the group, I want you to mirror.

Make sure to shift gradually, almost imperceptibly, in order to not make it seem like you're mocking people. No one should ever notice you're even playing the Mirror Game.

Toll worker gives you a big smile? Smile back equally big.

Person next to you standing up tall? Stand up equally tall.

Person sitting in the waiting room across from you tapping their foot? Subtly tap your foot, too.

The key here is subtlety. If someone knows you're mirroring them, you're not playing the game right.

Open your peripheral vision to the movements of the entire group, and then try to mirror as best you can.

You're not fighting your way through a faceless crowd anymore.

You're just another little ant, just like every other little ant.

Not special at all.

GAME 63:

FOLLOW THE LEADER

Follow the Leader is a classic kids' game, right? We jump, skip, and crawl behind some appointed leader. Now, when we're kids, we don't give it too much thought. We're just having fun. It would be surprising if kids were thinking, "Oh man, Charlie, hopping again? He's the worst."

They're just doing, which means they're having fun and not overthinking.

Let's get back to this playful kids' version of the game.

Here's how:

When you're driving or walking somewhere, I want you to pretend you're playing Follow the Leader. This is especially great when you're waiting in line or in traffic. I can't stress enough how important it is to not get caught. Subtlety is gonna be your best friend here. You really don't want anyone thinking you're making fun of them.

And then you just follow. If they're slow, you're slow.

If they're walking, you're walking.

If they're hurrying, you're hurrying.

If they're laughing, you're laughing.

Literally following the leader, and making someone who isn't you the boss, will help you take that hat of specialness off and become just another cog, just like every other totally not special cog.

GAME 64:

EXAGGERATION NATION

Imagine you're standing in a circle. One person moves his arms and says, "Whoosh." The next, without a nanosecond of hesitation, moves her arms the same way but a little bigger while saying, "Whoosh" louder. Then the next exaggerates the Whoosh and movement some more. And then more and more as the sound and movement go around the circle. By the time it gets back to the person who started the Whoosh, it's ridiculous, loud, and oh so much more than when we started.

It's like a game of Telephone. As you whisper the message to the next person, things change. Things get lost in translation and adjust with each individual who passes the message along.

Exaggeration Nation is similar to Follow the Leader, but I want you to bump up whatever the other person is doing.

Please continue to be subtle and not get caught. You are not making fun of anyone. You are joining in the fun. So if someone is yelling at his kid in front of you, don't choose that as the thing you exaggerate! Be cool, people. Be cool.

However, if someone is twirling her hair with her finger, exaggerate that shit!

Someone power posing with his hands on his hips? Exaggerate that pose!

Or if someone bops their head to the soothing Muzak on the elevator, exaggerate it!

Do what they're doing, but do it a little more, a little bigger, a little faster or slower, a little louder or quieter.

This is similar to finding the game. You are focusing on someone else and finding the game in what they're doing.

Again, it will help you focus on what other people are doing instead of how gosh darned special you are.

Because, once again (I really can't say it enough) . . . you're not.

GAME 65:

LEMMINGS

Lemmings may not actually follow each other to their deaths, but that's the rep they've been given. So we're going with it. Besides being adorable, I love the idea of little lemmings on their way to the edge of the cliff being all like, "Yay! Let's do this thing!"

Lemmings, or at least the folklore version of them, aren't bossy. They're team players to a serious fault.

That's why I want you to pretend you're a lemming. Don't follow anyone off a literal or metaphorical cliff. But do pretend you're adorable and a freakin' sweet team player.

This is great when you're one of many. When you're in your office cubicle. When you're on the train or bus or highway. When you're at the grocery store.

Look around and picture that everyone there is just a fuzzy, adorable, sweet-ass lemming.

Or, if you prefer meerkats, be a meerkat. They're also adorable and play well with others.

Jan in Marketing is a lemming just like you. Cute! When no one is looking, do a little lemming face to really get into it.

The plumber who showed up an hour late? He's a lemming just like you! Now that you both are finally united, enjoy being lemmings together. You are both furry and cute and magical.

Put a picture of a lemming up in your office or on your fridge to remind you that you're a fuzzy little worker bee. Lots of people have tiger paintings instead, but they think they're special. Lemmings totally don't. Be a lemming, man.

Lemmings get it. Meerkats get it. We're all in this together. Hmmm, I guess even *High School Musical* gets it.

GAME 66:

FIND THE RHYTHM

If I said there was a rhythm to life, a unifying tempo that keeps us all connected, would you think I was microdosing LSD?

Here's the thing. Music and rhythm are happening all around us, whether you like it or not. (And whether I'm microdosing or not.) So we can choose to embrace and explore it, or we can ignore it and grow old and die alone. Wow, I've made this a really tough choice, haven't I?

My daughter is really good at most of these games because she's a genius. (Actually, it's just because she's a baby. We're all born playful and curious.)

When Ella is toddling around the world, she is hearing things that I just don't hear. Everything is new to her, so she's excited to explore instead of being bored or annoyed.

Let's get back to that place where we're really listening while we move through our worlds!

Let's find the rhythm that's already happening all around us.

The crickets are chirping. The water is dripping. The feet are stomping. The dog is hacking. The heater is humming. The traffic is whirring.

Once you hear the noises, pause to try to get into the rhythm. The whir of my refrigerator has this even, quarter-note rhythm of loud to soft, loud to soft. Then on top of that, I can hear rattling in the ceiling, I think because of the AC. It adds a more irregular, percussive element.

Now that you can hear the rhythm for what it is, move your body to it. It doesn't have to be a full-on Martha Graham moment. I'm just swaying to my noisy house clatter, back and forth, back and forth.

You can do this on the street or at the office. Listen for the sounds caused by the people and objects around you. Then find the rhythm and move to it. You can tap your toes, sway, or bob your head.

There's something about knowing that we're rhythmically connected to each other that makes me know I'm actually a table lamp.

Ooops, that was a tell. I'm for sure microdosing.

GAME 67:

COG IN THE MACHINE

There's a game called Machine that is pretty common in Acting 101 classes the world over. Everyone stands in a big circle. Then one person goes to the center and does a repetitive sound and movement. They have to repeat this over and over and over, while, one by one, everyone in the circle joins in with a complimentary sound and movement. The idea is that the group is building something that functions as a whole.

Then the so-called machine can speed up and slow down, depending on the flights of fancy of the instructor or the group.

My favorite part is when the machine disbands and we talk about what the machine was. For some reason, I find naming the machine a really important part of the exercise. If you were really committed and involved in the machine, you should definitely have an idea, almost instinctual, about what it does.

Well, I'm just gonna say it. You are merely a cog in the machinery of mankind.

After you become a pro at Find the Rhythm, I want you to add this machine element. First, find the rhythm of the room. Then join in. Then decide what your machine is.

It might go something like this. You are sitting at your desk. It's a New Age open concept office, so there are other desks and people all around you. You listen. You hear pens scratching paper, the oscillation of the fan, the low murmur of voices. You close your eyes and begin rocking your legs back and forth in rhythm to your environment. You do this for fifteen seconds. Then open your eyes and name that machine. We are a steam engine!

Let's have another example, shall we?

Let's say you're at the ballpark. You know. The place where they play . . . ball. I don't know anything about sports, so this example might go off the rails at some point. Okay, you're at the ballpark. There is music and loud cheering with intermittent crescendos. You hear balls being hit by bats and hawkers selling their peanuts and Cracker Jacks. You close your eyes and clap along to the cacophony. You yell and clap for fifteen seconds then open your eyes. You were a rocket ship!

Now, you don't have to be machines that really exist. Maybe you try this game and can't pinpoint what actual machine you were. That's okay. You could be a Grass Petter or a Stomper Machine or an Ocean Maker. You know you're always going to get more points from me for creativity. So go nuts.

Here again, the aim of the game is to enjoy being one of many.

So close your eyes and join the machine instead of raging against it, you adorable little cog, you.

GAME 68:

COCKTAIL PARTY

I'm trash at small talk, networking, and cocktail parties, absolute rubbish. So if you're anything like me, here's a game to get you through.

The founders of the iO Theater write about an improv game called Cocktail Party.[4] In the game, three couples are spread out onstage, but close enough to be within earshot of each other. Each couple gets a different topic. Then they take turns small-talking about their various topics. As the game goes on, ideas from other couples' conversations naturally weave into the conversations of the other couples. It's pretty cool when it works well, and this idea of disparate topics weaving together is at the heart of improv, especially long-form improv.

But that Cocktail Party isn't going to help you at a real cocktail party without some adjustments.

Normally, I'm wedged against the wall at a party, somewhere between the grandfather clock and the back wall. I'm not making this up. Ask my husband about the time we went to Tim Gunn's apartment. That's where you could find me, instead of mixing and mingling with the celebrities who were, more logically, in the center of the room.

Come on! We can be so much more than wallflowers, friends!

While you're wedged against the clock, I want you to observe and listen to all the small-talkings going on around you. You could do this at a party, a networking event, a conference, or in the break room at work. Just listen and watch. There's no rush.

Now let the small talk and movements of the other people carry you into the room. If people look serious, be serious. If people are smiling, smile! If people are talking about the weather, turn to someone and just tell them what the hell the weather is today. "It is raining!" Just do what everyone else is doing.

Don't try to be smart. Don't be great. Don't even be good.

Just do what everyone else is doing.

I spend so much time thinking about how amazing I need to be, I never peel myself off that wall. Don't be like me. Do what everyone else is doing first. Then start talking about what-ever they're talking about.

Don't think. Just do.

Don't wedge yourself behind a grandfather clock all night. Take three minutes to observe the other guests. Then go!

GAME 69:

LET IT GO . . . LET IT GO

Sorry to get that old gem stuck in your head again, but it's a good mantra to keep in mind when you're super-set on how the conversation is going to go. Let it go. Let it go!

There was an old *Saturday Night Live* skit where a man was chatting with a couple of his friends. He was always about three topics behind, though. If his friends talked about the weather, then sports, then last night, he was just getting to the weather.

This game would have been perfect for him.

Instead of getting stuck on how you have to talk about your new house or your dog or your boyfriend or tell that new joke, let it go. This takes constant practice. When you catch yourself not really listening and thinking about what you're going to say next, just let it go. I also remind myself that it's not about me.

I have to play this game an embarrassing amount. I have that bad but extremely common habit of making every con-versation about me. If my best friend tells me about her boyfriend, I feel compelled to tell her about my relationship. If an acquaintance tells me about how stressful it was at the doctor's office, I retort with a doctor's office story of my own. If my sister tells me about something cute her kid did, I respond with something cute my kid did. These are normal, appropriate responses . . . if you're a narcissist!

People I talk to aren't fishing to hear more about me. They are talking about themselves. And just like we learned in physics or kindergarten or wherever, a body in motion wants to stay in motion. They want to keep talking about themselves.

So let go of what you want to say about yourself and learn more about them.

When you get stuck on yourself or on how the convo should go, let that go, too. And let the conversation go where someone else wants for a change.

GAME 70:

THE QUESTION GAME

My mom struggles to speak up for herself. She wants everyone to be happy, so she's not likely to cause a fuss, even if that means not telling the truth. We were on vacation, and I noticed she wasn't eating, so I asked her how her lunch was.

She said, "Fine."

This isn't my first rodeo. Her lunch wasn't fine, so I asked another question. I didn't repeat the same question, which is what people often do.

I asked her a creative follow-up. "Would you order that seafood risotto again?"

She said, "No."

When I asked why not, she said the risotto was under-cooked, and she didn't care for mussels.

With my creative questioning, I got to the truth. We were able to have a fantastic lunch after that—when I ended up sharing mine with her.

People withhold the truth or just tidbits about themselves all the time for myriad reasons. Make it your job to ask those creative questions to learn more about them.

Ask what food they would eat if they had to eat one food for the rest of their life. Ask which character they would play in the film you just saw and why. When they say they're having a good day, ask them why.

Asking creative and authentic (you have to actually give a shit) questions deepens conversations and keeps the focus on the person you're talking to. That's where it needs to be.

Don't ping-pong, switching the focus between you and the person you're talking to. Go deep.

And just like that, you have made things about someone else, someone who isn't you. You've broken the old habit of thinking only about yourself and your own specialness.

And I think that selflessness is actually pretty special. See how that works? You're more special now because you know you're not.

Maybe your mama should have explained it like that. You are special only when you make others special.

But now you know, so continue to treat others like the geniuses, poets, and artists they are. I'll even let you congratulate yourself for it.

TIME-OUT:
LET'S TALK ABOUT YOUR DRINKING

Did all that talk about your not being special make you want to reach for that glass of rosé?

We need to talk again.

Drinking is a way to numb our emotions. Drinking numbs us from strong feelings, be they good or bad. Obviously, I don't want you to have to be numb in order to play these games. The real aim is for you to play the games and deal with the sometimes strong feelings they bring up.

But alcoholism isn't going to be cured by playing some games. We all know that. Alcoholism is real. It's a disease. It destroys lives. My own dad died of it. Real talk.

So if your drinking is a problem, I hope you get

---

the very real help you very really need. If drinking isn't a problem for you, then abstain as you play these games anyway.

It's the same story for other drugs, even the caffeine in coffee. Now, I'm certainly no teetotaler, unless teetotaler means someone who has done some hardcore shit in his day. But if you want to get the most out of these games, I'd like you to try them sober.

Can't sober up? I repeat, please get the help you need and deserve. We want you back in the mix, showing up center stage with your heart and mind open. Get the help you need to kick the drugs first.

Put the mimosa down and proceed.

LESSON 8
Shut Up and Listen

Y ou can't improvise without being a good listener. And good listening is also clutch for a good life.

Often the reason we aren't good listeners is because we're stuck in our own heads, thinking about ourselves. "What do they think of me?" "How am I doing?" "Do I have something stuck in my teeth?" "When should I tell them the baseball anecdote?" "How's my hair?" "Do they like me?"

Those selfish thoughts prevent us from deep, truly engaged listening. They also cause us to miss all sorts of information.

In improv, thoughts like this make us miss what our character's name is and where we are. This is vital information!

In everyday life, these thoughts make us miss other people's names and where they work. Also vital information!

Practicing our listening skills can help us focus less on ourselves. A win! It's a shortcut to thinking less about ourselves and quieting our minds.

Clay Drinko, PhD

If it would work to just tell you to think less about yourself, I'd do it, but paradoxically, telling you to think less about yourself usually makes you think more about yourself.

So let's just focus on listening, a so-called soft skill with some hard-core benefits that will help us live a much more joyous and connected life.

GAME 71:

BREATHING, NOT BANTERING

We tend to fill every silent space with . . . well, not silence.

Silence makes most people uncomfortable. It gives us the time to start those negative, all-about-me thoughts. When someone isn't talking, usually people start thinking about what to say next.

But there's another way. Instead of bantering, filling every single second with word babble, just breathe. Challenge yourself to not think about what to say next or why no one is talking. Just be. Just breathe.

This is a good first step to breaking the habit of thinking instead of listening.

As you breathe, listen. There are still noises happening in the so-called silence.

Listen to the AC, to the traffic, to the music.

Someone will talk again someday. I promise.

It's gonna be okay.

130

GAME 72:

THE NAME GAME

The cheese may stand alone here, but one of my all-time fa-vorite movies is *The House Bunny* starring Anna Faris. My fa-vorite scene is where Shelley teaches the girls her trick to learn people's names. She just repeats their name in this low, grav-elly, demon voice. It's real stupid, but it makes me laugh every time.

Turns out, Shelley Darlington is onto something when it comes to listening and learning names. Repeating names a few times in different contexts helps us learn people's names. And with a demon voice, I'm assuming we learn them even faster.

So let's all be like Shelley, the *Playboy* Playmate with a heart of gold! When you meet someone new, repeat their name five times. Make it a game. Maybe something like this.

"Hi, I'm Tom."

"Tom?"

"Yes."

"Tom, it's great to meet you. Where do you work, Tom?"

"Google."

"Tom! I'm obsessed with that. I google stuff all the time. Be honest, Tom. Have you ever googled yourself?"

That's already five times! I'm much more likely to know Tom's name the next time I see him. Also, by repeating his name so many times so quickly, I've made the conversation all about Tom, which is another key to better listening.

So get out there and meet some new people. Repeat their names liberally.

Demon voice optional.

GAME 73:

PAUSE AND REFLECT (1-2-3)

It seems counterintuitive to be telling you to pause and reflect in a book about improv games, but in order to practice our listening skills, I want us to get in the habit of digesting what others are saying. Think of it as training wheels. Once you beef up those listening skills, you can stop pausing and reflecting and just ride.

But in the meantime, when you're conversing with someone, I want you to take a three-count after they say something. This will prevent you from interrupting or bulldozing your own conversation agenda into the mix.

During the three-count, repeat what they've just said in your head. Really think about what the person has told you. Only then, after the three-count, can you respond, but the response has to be about what they've just told you. You cannot change the subject. Just pause, reflect, and respond to what they just said.

It sounds simple, but pausing for three counts is a long time. Reflecting on what they said and not on yourself can be tricky. You can't think about whether or not you have something stuck in your teeth or a rogue nose hair.

But if you actually think about what they just said, the payoff is a better retort from you. Better listening makes for better conversations.

By pausing and reflecting, the goal is for you to really hear what they're saying and then for you to respond in kind.

It will also help you to stop interrupting, which is a definite bonus.

GAME 74:

RINSE AND REPEAT

If you can't repeat the last thing someone said, you probably weren't listening.

So that's exactly what I want you to do. When someone says something, start by repeating the last thing they said.

Let's have an example.

Let's say someone says, "My mom isn't feeling well. I'm worried that she might be really sick."

You would start your response with something like, "You're worried your mom might be really sick."

I think you'll be amazed at how this simple repetition can be enough to keep the other person engaged in the conversation. Repetition helps people feel heard, and that tends to keep them talking.

Sometimes just repeating what someone has said is enough to keep the conversation going. Sometimes you'll need to ask a follow-up question or get some clarification, but those are other games.

And they go something like . . .

GAME 75:

CLARIFICATION NATION

Are you sure that's what you heard? People often experience the same conversation very differently from the person they're talking to. They think they heard one thing. They add their own subtext. They assume and react. It's pretty normal human behavior. But it also causes a lot of unnecessary drama.

There's an easy way to stop this confusion before it ruins your marriage or any other important relationship. Double-check. Get confirmation of what was said and what was meant.

I want you to confirm what someone else said at least three times today. That's the game.

If someone says, "I wish you'd let me talk more," you can clarify, "You're saying I talk too much?"

Then let them explain and clarify. You might be right, or you might be wrong, but the act of clarifying gets you on the same page as whoever you're talking to.

Language is imprecise. We use words to try to express ideas, but language often falls short.

The best thing we can do in the face of this is to confirm that we're on the same page as the person we're speaking with.

It doesn't hurt to ask, "So you're saying . . . ?"

When you're back on the same page, then the conversation can continue.

Marriage saved. Divorce papers ripped up.

You're welcome.

GAME 76:

REPEATING THE NOTEWORTHY

There's a gem of goodness in every conversation.

That's what I want you to believe.

Now that you believe that, I need you to be the treasure hunter, always questing for that gem of goodness.

Try it at least once today. While you're conversing with someone, pick out the most magical, interesting, profound, important thing they've said.

Then repeat it. Without comment. Just like you're repeating some good shit Confucius said once.

To listen for the good stuff means you're listening.

What the other person does when you repeat their words without comment is up to them.

GAME 77:

HARD-HITTING REPORTER

I want you to pretend you're motherfuckin' Diane Sawyer or Oprah, or if you're super old-school, Barbara Walters. You are a hard-hitting reporter, and you want to get some dirt on this person. In fact, you want them to lay their soul bare. You want them to spill the tea, reveal all, and hopefully cry a single tear from their right eye. Go in, girl!

The common magic of these hard-hitting reporters? Follow-up questions.

Too many times people just nod their heads or agree or talk about themselves. They don't dig for the deeper layers of that onion.

If someone tells you their dog died, don't just say you're sorry. Barbara Walters would ask that dog's name and how long they had him and what happened on the day that he died. She would go in!

If someone says they don't get along with their brother, don't say that you don't get along with yours either. Hell, no! Oprah would ask when the relationship went south. She would ask what their biggest regret was and how they have tried to heal that rift. She would go hard!

If someone says they're nervous for the future, don't just say "Uh-huh" or "I bet." Diane Sawyer would drink an over-flowing glass of chianti and then ask them to describe their freakin' doomsday scenario and when in their childhood they started to feel that way. She would take no prisoners!

Go in and go hard and take no prisoners. Don't be afraid to ask the hard-hitting questions.

GAME 78:

SUMMARIZE SURPRISE

When I was teaching middle and high school English, one of my tricks to see if someone had read and understood something was to simply ask them to summarize it. Summarizing is actually a much more difficult skill than repeating. You can parrot something back without really having any idea what it means, but to summarize something means you have absorbed it and decided what's most important.

Imagine if someone could summarize everything you said. Wouldn't you just feel listened-to as hell?

That's what I want you to do. The next time you strike up a conversation with someone, I want you to summarize what they've said. Pick out the most important bits and edit what they've just said into a succinct little blurb.

You can start with, "So you're saying . . ." or "Let me get this straight . . ."

The important part is to show them that you fully get what they're saying. Just like with Clarification Nation, they might tell you you're wrong. You're still totally winning just for playing.

Just by summarizing, you have showed that you're aiming for some hard-core deep listening.

GAME 79:

YOU PROBABLY THINK THIS GAME IS ABOUT YOU

I don't know how many different ways I can say this, but it's just not about you. If you're making things about you, you're not making them about others, and I think that sucks.

This is a three-strikes-and-you're-out game.

When you're having a conversation with someone, I want you to track the times you make things all about you.

They tell a story, you tell a similar story about you. Strike one.

They ask for advice, you tell them what you *personally* would do. Strike two.

They talk about how work is going, you talk about how work's going for you. Strike three. You're out.

When you're out, you have to apologize for making everything about you. You have to own up to the fact that you keep making everything about you.

Now, what is there to talk about if you can't talk about yourself?

If you're seriously asking me that, you haven't been paying attention.

Talk about them. Ask them questions. Get clarification. Summarize and go deeper with what they're saying.

Some conversations can be about you . . . later. But I want you to first be able to allow them to be about someone else.

Once you master this selfless skill, you can go back to talking about yourself, but I think you'll find that there are appropriate and inappropriate times to do so.

When it's about them, it's about them. When it's about you, it's about you.

Don't confuse the two.

And for now, it's one, two, three strikes you're out at the old convo game.

Play ball!

GAME 80:

GOLD STAR DAY

Did you ever see that Judi Dench movie where she's an old lesbian schoolmarm, *Notes on a Scandal*? If you haven't, you must.

Basically, Judi Dench is obsessed with Cate Blanchett. I mean, who wouldn't be? Cate's character sleeps with a student, an obvious no-no. Judi's character keeps this crazy diary detailing her lesbian obsession with Cate's character, and she marks days as gold star days when Cate is especially alluring. I mean, that's what I remember. It's been a long time since the movie came out.

Either way, the important takeaway from the movie is that Judi Dench and Cate Blanchett can act their faces off.

And that the idea of having gold star days is appealing.

As you go through your humdrum days, I want you to open your eyes and ears and be on the lookout for what makes every day a gold star day. Then write it in your journal.

Listen carefully when people talk to you, then write their gold star ideas and phrases in your journal.

If you're primed for gold star words, you're going to hear them when they're said.

You don't have to be a crazy old lesbian schoolmarm to work that journal and have gold star days. Listen carefully, and make each conversation gold star–worthy.

We take listening for granted. Most people think they're good listeners, but they're not. Put your phone down and stop thinking about yourself. Ask the other person to go deeper. Ask for clarification when you need to. Do everything in your power to listen carefully to what people are saying to you. Only then will you be ready to agree, agree, agree.

It's time to start lowering our defenses—by saying yes.

LESSON 9

Yaaas!

Arguably the most famous improv rule is "Yes, And." When one improviser says something, their scene partner is supposed to agree with that reality, and then add something new to the scene.

Adhering to the "Yes, And" rule would mean that if your partner says, "Hey honey, I'm home," you would say something like "Welcome back, sweety! I made your favorite for dinner, meatloaf."

Breaking the "Yes, And" rule might mean you say something like "I've never met you before in my life" or "This isn't my house."

People have a tendency to say no because it makes them feel safer. If I shut down your idea, I don't have to go on a wild ride into the unknown with you. I know how the scene ends when I say no. It ends immediately!

Yes helps scenes keep going. It prevents confusion and argument. But we have to quiet down some old defense mechanisms in order to say yes. We can't feel compelled to be better or right. We can't be defensive or scared. We truly have to be open to traveling into the unknown with another person, sharing every idea along the way.

A caveat about "Yes, And": obviously, saying yes to everything is problematic. There are many times when you should definitely say no in life. And for women, LGBTQIA people, and people of color, yes can be especially fraught. In a rape culture, in an iniquitous society, saying no is often the only thing you can do to protect yourself. As we play around with the "Yes, And" rule, I want to make it very clear from the beginning that I'm not telling everyone to say yes to everything no matter what. When you're in a safe place, where saying yes doesn't put you at risk or force you to give up your ideals, then you can say yes. Trust yourself. Know yourself. Then decide whether or not you want to say yes.

And remember that "Yes, And" doesn't mean literally always saying yes. It means going along with someone else's ideas . . . when it feels safe and right for you.

So let's stop shutting down every idea that comes our way. Let's see what happens when we start saying yes. Let's go along with other people's ideas and see where we end up.

GAME 81:

JUST NOD YOUR HEAD

I don't know about you, but I can be super-defensive and quite the contrarian. I was so quick to say no that my dad's nickname for me growing up was "dumb ass." He would always say that if he said the sky was blue, I would say it was black. Once, when I wasn't looking, he changed the name on my homework from "Clay" to "dumb ass." When I told the teacher that my dad did it, she wasn't buying it.

I think there's a place for skepticism and playing devil's advocate, but that place is not while we're brainstorming or chitchatting with the neighbors.

I tend to get stuck in this no, no, no rut, and it doesn't earn me a lot of friends, or any seats of honor at dinner parties.

More often than not, just going along with ideas will get us much farther. It helps us see the merit in what other people are saying. It helps us listen and makes others feel like we're listening to them and really honoring what they're saying. And remember that you're not committing to anything long-term. Just living the spirit of openness.

So to begin to break that no, no, no habit, I want you to practice nodding your head yes, yes, yes.

You need to clock ten up-and-down head nods every time you talk to anyone. That's it! That's the game. Nod ten times.

Just note how that head nodding feels. Does it feel uncomfortable? Would you rather be shaking your head no? Or does it feel natural?

Simply nodding our heads yes can impact how we think. The more you nod yes, the easier it will eventually be to start *saying* yes—and even mean it.

Look at that. Yes, yes, yes! We're on our way.

GAME 82:

A THOUSAND TIMES NO

Before we get too far into this *yes* thing, let's get some *nos* out of our system. I want you to see just how often your instinct is no, when it could just as easily be yes.

I want you to count how many times you shake your head no or flat out say "no" to someone today. In a one-hour period, I want you to tally those nos. That's gonna be your "shut 'em down" ratio, the number of times you shut things down per hour.

Now try it again. Try to lower your "shut 'em down" ratio in the next hour.

At first, it's going to be tough even noticing every time you say no, but after a couple rounds, I think you'll start to recognize that you have a problem, a no problem.

But fear not. The first step toward recovery is admitting that there's a problem.

And yes, we have a big no problem.

GAME 83:

A THOUSAND TIMES YES

All you have to do today is say yes! I want you to think yes, yes, yes, and say it any and every time you can.

Your coworker asks if you want to grab a coffee. Yes, you do. That's one point.

Your husband tells you his latest ideas about work. Yes, those are helpful. That's two points.

Your mom tells you that you've always been ungrateful. Yes, it's something you should really work on. That's three points! Who cares if your mother is slowly killing your spirit?!

Now, don't go saying yes when it's for real bad news. Don't lie or do drugs or give consent when you don't want to. Safety first. And integrity a close second.

But I do think there are tons of times in your day when you say no instead of giving things a chance.

And that's what this game is all about. Rack up those yeses.

Then, when you wake up tomorrow, try to rack up even more.

Fun?

Why . . . yes, of course it is.

GAME 84:

THE CLAP

When someone claps at anything I've said, I feel like a rock star. Clapping is solo high-fiving, and it's important. So listen up.

We don't clap for each other enough. That changes today.

When someone announces an idea, innovation, or inspiration, just clap your hands. And no sarcastic slow claps. You gotta really mean it.

"Let's go to the park." Clap your hands.

"We could branch out and sell cupcakes." Clap those hands.

"Why don't we start seeing other people?" Well, it's an idea, so clap away.

You're not necessarily going along with the idea, or even saying it's amazing. You're just rewarding every idea that is born, in real time.

The world needs more ideas, not fewer. And anytime we don't clap for a new idea, future idea fairies don't get their wings. And also Tinker Bell dies . . . or something.

So use your best judgment, and clap away.

GAME 85:

YES PEOPLE

Yes People get a bad rap. People say they're sucking up or that they don't have thoughts in their own heads. I say they know something most people don't.

There's power in going along with other people's ideas. It helps spark group creativity. A brainstorm sesh (that's millennial for "session") with a lot of No Men is going nowhere fast, man.

But when people let go of their own egos enough to say yes, ideas really start to flow. People feel more comfortable sharing. It becomes a happening, creative atmosphere . . . or should I say "at-less-fear." Oooh, see what I did there? The creativity can't be tamed!

So now I want you to become a Yes Man or a Yes Woman or a Yes Person.

Here's your script. I want you to say, "Nice!" or "Uh-huh, tell me more!" or "Cool! I love it!" Have a handful of affirmative responses at the ready.

Then the next time someone drops an idea bomb your way, bump, set, and spike their shit with one of your "Yeah, I love it!" responses.

"Next season is all about skirts."

"Tell me more!"

"We have to cut some benefits."

"Cool. Go on with your bad self!"

"I'm going to marry Kanye West."

"Yes, girl. Get it every way you got it. I'm obsessed with what you're throwing down!"

I think you get the picture.

GAME 86:

SENTENCE STARTERS

Before yessing becomes second nature, I want to give you some sentence starters. These work wonders in the classroom.

A fourteen-year-old forgets how to enter your classroom politely? Give him a sentence starter like "Pardon me, may I please . . ."

A high school senior yells, "You're a moron!" Give her a sentence starter like "While I see the merits of your idea, I have to disagree because . . ."

Sentence starters help us rewire our brains with better habits, habits like positivity and active listening.

So to beef up your yes game, I want you to keep two sentence starters close at hand. "That's a good idea . . ." and "I like how you/he/she/they said . . ."

Maybe that's all you say. You are winning because you're agreeing with someone else's reality. You're seeing their point of view, which makes them feel seen, heard, and valued. So good on you.

Maybe you're then able to add something else. "That's a good idea. We could also add a jingle." Or "I like what you said. I can give that a second look to make sure the wording is just right."

It's hard not to be a team player when you're a standout cheerleader.

All you need is a "Yes, And" starter, and the rest will take care of itself.

GAME 87:

YES

The "Yes, And" game is really at the heart of all things improv. I remember drilling this exercise at every single rehearsal. So how does it work?

Two people meet in the middle of the playing space. One is person A and one B. Person A initiates the scene (just a fancy way of saying starts). The initiation is the phrase that starts to build the world. Maybe "This lava is hot" or "My pitching arm is killing me."

Now it's person B's turn. Person B has to literally say yes. Then they repeat what person A said in a way that makes sense in conversation. To continue with our two super-subpar examples, "Yes, this lava is hot" or "Yes, your pitching arm is killing you."

Person B continues by saying the word "and" and then

adding new information. But I want to stop here because this lesson is all about "yes." We'll get to "and" in Lesson 10.

So this game is just called Yes because I only want you to respond to people with "Yes" and then the repetition of what they just said.

For example, if someone says, "I've missed you!" You say, "Yes, you've missed me" and then go from there. Once you start nailing this yessing, you could make it flow better in conversation with some therapy-type words like "I see that you've missed me" or "I can tell you've missed me."

Let's say someone says, "You never listen." You would say, "Yes, I never listen." But where do you go from there? You could say that it's something you want to work on or something you're sorry about. And then look what you just did! You proved that jerk wrong! You do listen. And you're positive and fantastic. Good on you, again.

This kind of yes then repeating can be a little clunky, but I want you to force the habit. It's the calisthenics that will make you listen better and build off other people's realities, instead of holding on to your own lonely reality with your sad-face buzzard talons.

It starts with yes and some repetition.

Where it goes from there, no one knows. And that's a good thing.

GAME 88:

RIGHT THE WRONG, YES THE NO

Now that you're becoming quite the "Yes Expert," it's time for you to start spreading that knowledge. You know, pay it forward and all that.

The next time you hear someone shoot down someone else's idea, I want you to try to salvage the situation. I want you to try to yes what's already been noed.

Let's have an example, shall we?

Let's say you're having another brainstorm sesh at work. And let's say Steve says that he thinks the new campaign should involve rainbows and butterflies. So far so good. But then Damien says, "That's a terrible idea. I hate it!"

Uh oh.

Besides buying Damien a copy of this book for his birthday, which you should also do, you can try to remedy the pain, undo the no, and save your office!

You might say, "I like butterflies and rainbows" or "Rainbows? Butterflies? Tell me more, Steve."

Now you've got some positive vibes running through the meeting.

This might get the ideas flowing again.

It might save Steve some hurt feelings.

It might piss off Damien.

Either way, you can't have a truly creative space without some yesses.

Sorry, Damien, but someone had to be the hero.

GAME 89:

HAVE YOUR CAKE
AND EAT IT, TOO

Bravely noing after someone else yesses is one approach, and it's a fine approach at that. But the other way to go is to try to yes both contradictory opinions. It's time to try to yes everybody, and their mamas, too.

The next time you find yourself in between two contrasting opinions, I want you to yes both parties.

Let's say you're back at that brainstorming sesh. Gina thinks that the company website is woefully outdated. Jill, who was in charge of updating said website, thinks it's fine, funky, fresh, and current. What are you to do?

Well, you're going to try to yes everyone. You might say that you really like the website, especially the font choices, but you also think it could use some freshening up, especially how it looks on mobile platforms. Look at you go! When once you couldn't yes anyone, now you're yessing literally everyone. You can't be tamed. You are a miracle.

Do notice what happens when you yes contrasting opinions. I think you'll feel better, the room's mood will lighten, and everyone will get much more work done in a much more collaborative way.

Now, that's something to say yes to.

GAME 90:

DEFENSES DOWN

I'm a really defensive person. When my husband asks how my day was, I'm likely to hear, "Seems like you didn't accomplish much today, loser."

Whoa, whoa, whoa there, kiddo. That is not what he said. That kind of defensive insecurity can be really harmful to relationships. It's for sure unfair to the other person involved. Plus, it's just downright exhausting to be so "in your own head" all the time.

So let's try to bring those defenses down a tad.

After yessing and head-nodding your way through this lesson, I hope you're more primed to start with agreeing, with seeing the other person's truth first. For this game—and it's not going to be easy—I want you to totally put the walls down. When someone says something negative about you, perceived or real, I want you to agree with them first and foremost.

"You're so slow."

"I know. I'm always dawdling."

"You aren't going to apply for that job, are you?"

"I could see how this job isn't in my wheelhouse."

"You're bad at sex."

"There's certainly room for improvement, eh?"

Coming back without defensiveness can be disarming. People are often looking to start some shit with you, whether consciously or unconsciously. People love them some drama. But by lowering your walls and being open to even the harshest criticism, you more than meet the other person halfway. It's hard to fight with someone who's already on your side.

Now, if someone goes beyond criticism into abuse, then do not play this game with them. Get help. Leave if it's safe to do so. Always, your safety and self-worth come first.

But if someone you trust lobs a truthball your way, I want you to hit it out of the park by admitting that it's a truthball. Or at least finding *some* truth in their perspective.

You can't hit a truthball anywhere if you can't admit that it's a truthball in the first place.

Stop being defensive, and start really taking that tough criticism.

Now that you're better at starting with yes, at agreeing and finding the common ground first, I hope you're less defensive and more open to other people's truths.

But that's just the first half of "Yes, And."

After we agree, we need to add onto other people's realities. We need to keep interactions going by adding onto what others are dishing out.

It's time to start anding.

LESSON 10
And What?

You can yes all day long, but that still does not a good conversation make. Yesses are what set us up for a positive interaction, but "ands" are the actual conversation. Without ands, it's a one-sided affair, and no one wants a one-sided affair.

The idea behind the "And" in the "Yes, And" improv rule is that we need to add onto the reality the other person initiated. If they say they're a dentist, we can say that we like how they renovated their new office. If they say we're bowling, we can say that last time we bowled we both got perfect scores. If they say we're dinosaurs, we can say that we're in Jurassic Park.

These simple little ands pack a big cumulative punch. Every time we and each other, the scene becomes a little more filled out, and clearer to the audience. Our relationship begins to have a history and some emotional heft. Both improvisers and the audience can really begin to imagine the location. Eventually, with hundreds of ands, we have a scene that feels complete and satisfying.

I want this for your everyday scenes, too!

Instead of passively listening or, conversely, hogging the spotlight, I want you to share the airtime. These And Games will help you add onto what's already going on.

And I think that's going to really enhance your everyday interactions with people.

"And" on that note, let's play.

GAME 91:

SAY ANYTHING

Before we get too deep into what makes a good "and," I want you to just start willy-nilly anding people. I call this game Say Anything, and that's exactly what you're going to do.

Imagine you're a Kardashian. (Don't overthink it!)

At least three times in the next twenty-four hours, you have to follow up your yessing with an anding, and any anding will do. See Lesson 9 for more on how to yes.

Let's say someone tells you they were just visiting their in-laws in Toronto. You start by agreeing with their reality. Maybe you say, "Yes! Toronto" or "Mmmmhmmmm, in-laws."

Now, that's a good start, but it's not going to keep the conversation moving forward. Some people need a little help to keep talking.

So let's and them with something. Say anything!

Maybe you follow up "Yes! Toronto" with "it's pretty there in the winter" or "the New York City of Canada!" Don't worry about it being good. Just add a new talk nugget after your initial yes.

Let's round it out with our "Mmmmmhmmmmm, in-laws" example. You could say, "I, too, have in-laws" or "I've seen *Monster-in-Law* starring Jennifer Lopez and Jane Fonda."

Not great. But hey, at least it's something.

As long as you and by saying anything at least three times today, you're good to go.

We can talk about what makes an exquisite and later.

For now, just Say Anything.

GAME 92:

EXPERT

Anytime a game involves lying, I'm all in.

This isn't necessarily bald-faced lying, but it's certainly not getting hung up on the truth . . . or facts . . . or even reality as most people understand it.

It's called Expert.

The improv game goes like this. Everyone stands in a circle. Someone announces an academic topic, maybe geology or the space race. Then one by one, players go to the center to pretend to be the expert on that topic. The aim is to be convincing, not necessarily accurate. Now, you're not trying to be funny and make stuff up. If you really are an expert in aerospaceology, then no need to make anything up, right? But if you're not, you need to stand tall, be confident, and sell us on it.

Now, no one is giving you weird academic topics in real life, so here's how we're going to play Expert on the daily.

Often we're worried about making mistakes, about saying something stupid or inaccurate. We have to let that go for this game. It's better to keep the convo moving than to be perfect.

So the next time you're having a conversation, pick out a topic that has come up. I don't care if it's hedge funds, nuclear fusion, or tarantulas. You're going to speak on it!

Let me lead by example. Let's actually use those three examples.

Hedge funds. "Where do I start? Elite investors go with these firms in order to get the highest returns and try to beat the market. I agree with Warren Buffett, though. I think a simple index fund, especially value stocks, can earn more over time."

I don't know how accurate I am, but I'm doing my best. I'm not making jokes about hedgehogs or changing the subject. I'm owning it. And if I'm wrong, I'm sure someone will correct me, and that's totally acceptable.

Nuclear fusion. "When plutonium atoms get accelerated, their electrons become unstable and fuse together with uranium. The scientists behind the atomic bomb had no idea they were making the bomb that would kill so many."

Okay, I'm for sure wrong here. I have no idea what nuclear

fusion is, and I don't super care. But I tried my best and used what I do know or what I kind of think I might know.

Tarantulas. "Definitely an eight-legged, furry spider. They get pretty large, especially the ones in the Sahara. They are not insects or mammals. They are arachnids."

I think I have some hits and misses here. I got weirdly specific with the Sahara, so that could have been a misstep, but I confidently did my best. So I win the Expert game!

I don't recommend playing this game when the stakes are high, when accuracy matters. Don't play Expert with your boss.

But with people you're comfortable around, play away. They might call you on your BS, but the fact that you're propelling the conversation forward is worth more than accuracy.

We're not playing *Jeopardy* here. We're playin' motherfuckin' life!

GAME 93:

OFFICE PARTY (AND WE COULD)

People tend to confuse brainstorming with judging ideas. They're two very different processes. Brainstorming is pure ideation; the more ideas, the merrier. After brainstorming is complete, and we have as many ideas as humanly imaginable, only then can we start to evaluate each idea's merits and start eliminating and changing ideas.

I'm not 100 percent sure why I thought Office Party was

a good name for this next game, but I'm keeping it. Maybe because it will make your office feel more like a party. Maybe I was microdosing again.

Either way, it should help your creativity, brainstorming, and collaboration.

The next time someone shares an idea, I want you to add onto that idea. Keep it going. I prefer the sentence starter "And we could . . ."

Let's say Bev in Marketing thinks we should use a mascot. Yes, Bev, you are an angel! And we could put the mascot on shirts and bags. The mascot could be a troll or a robot! You don't even have to like Bev's idea. But the anding has the magical power of turning shit ideas into passable ones. You're welcome, Bev!

Now let's say Dwayne in Corporate thinks everyone should bring their dogs to work like all the time. Yes, Dwayne! You are a whisper of innovation in an otherwise stale cesspool of an office! Even if you hate dogs, hate the idea, hate Dwayne, just go right along with it and add, "And we could turn the copy room into a doggy social hour at five p.m."

Be careful not to make fun of people with your anding. Stick with their idea; don't list other adjacent ones. If you responded to Dwayne by saying we should also bring babies, cats, and in-laws, you've clearly derailed his suggestion by taking it too far and turning it into something else. You don't want to do that.

You really want to try to add onto the original idea and make it better.

This habit of trying to make other people's ideas better, instead of hearing them all as competition against your idea, will help improve the mood of your next interminable meeting.

It will also help you see seeds of greatness in ideas, instead of instinctively shooting them all down.

GAME 94:

YES AND

We're back to the heartland of improv, the "Yes And" exercise. In Lesson 9, we did the first half of this "Yes And" game. Now it's time to put it all together.

When someone says something in conversation, you must respond with a yes if it makes any worldly sense. Then you repeat what they said, changing pronouns as necessary.

Then you add on. This is the "And" part. You literally say, "And," and then add a new detail to the reality that the other person started creating. You don't bring up a new topic or change the topic to yourself. You add onto what the other person said and you just yessed and repeated.

Let's say someone tells you they were thinking about moving. You could say, "Yes, you're thinking of moving. And I know a great moving company." Or "And it's cheaper to move in the middle of the month."

You want to avoid questions, and avoid changing the subject.

The yes helps you agree with their reality. The repetition helps you actively listen. But it's the and that helps you propel the conversation forward.

Sometimes it feels like I'm having two different conversations with someone, mine and theirs. "Yes, And" helps get us on the same page.

It's not a competition. It's a conversation.

So yes it. Repeat it. And it.

GAME 95:

YES AND, YES BUT, NO

"Yes, And"ing someone can be clunky and awkward. But hey, we're trying to break old habits and set new neural pathways here.

I want to try an experiment for all you "Yes, And" non-believers.

Today, I want you to tackle three separate conversations with three wildly different approaches.

You're going to "Yes, And" in one conversation. See the previous game for more details, but the gist is this: You agree with what someone else said by literally saying, "Yes." Then you repeat what they just said, changing pronouns to make it make sense. Then you say, "And," and add a new, related detail to the conversation. Don't change the subject and don't ask questions.

Then see how it goes. Does the conversation keep flowing? What's the mood? How are you feeling after using "Yes, And"?

In another conversation, I want you to try "Yes, But." It starts the same as "Yes, And," but instead of saying "and," you're going to say "but" and then add to the conversation.

Maybe they say they're late for work. You could say, "Yes, you're late for work. But I thought you didn't even like that job."

How did "Yes, But" go? Does the conversation flow? What's the mood? How are you feeling?

Finally, I want you to "No" a conversation. No need for repeating. Just shut it down! Let's say someone says they're repaving Route 209. You would just say, "No." And then wait.

Notice how things go. What's the conversation like? The general mood? Your mood?

These games can be awkward even in an improv rehearsal, so, again, I don't want you to risk high-stakes conversations with this experiment. Don't "No" your boss. Don't "Yes, But" at a job interview. Try these three out when the stakes are low, or you could explain what you were doing after the fact if need be.

I think you'll find that "Yes, And" keeps things on topic and chugging along better than "Yes, But"—and way better than "No."

I know I've made you a human guinea pig, but I think it's important for you to experience this for yourself.

Then think about all the times in your life you've inadvertently "Yes, But"ed and "No"ed.

Let this experiment be a turning point where you start "Yes, And"ing as much as you can.

GAME 96:

CIRCLE OF
THE CONVERSATION

Improv pioneer Keith Johnstone often talked about staying within the circle of a story.[1]

I think about this concept almost every time people start telling anecdotes in conversation.

The idea is pretty simple. If you're making up a story and it involves a bear, a tree, and some honey, then you shouldn't introduce a robot at the eleventh hour. You need to stay within the circle of the story. In other words, use what you've already got.

Now, this is a fun party game to make up a story from scratch. It's especially fun for kids, but I want you to stay within the circle of your conversations, too.

When I'm talking to someone, I often have this little voice burrow into my head that says, "Ooooh oooh, talk about this other unrelated thing."

Then I spend the next few moments thinking about how to weave in my own conversational agenda.

Well, spoiler alert: that whole time I was spending thinking about how I wanted to hijack the conversation, I was not actually listening to what was going on.

So I want you to let all that go next time. Don't let that voice burrow anywhere near your bean!

Instead, listen carefully to where the conversation is IRL. And then simply stay within that circle.

If people are talking about the last election and where the local polling place is, you're limited in what you can talk about. Don't bring up your marital problems!

If people are talking about fishing and a family reunion, don't talk about work! That's just not where the conversation is.

Now, I'm not saying you can never for the rest of your life change the subject, but I want you to feel the magic of exhausting a topic, of exploring topics more deeply, and of keeping people talking instead of hijacking conversations.

All you have to do is stay within that circle. No robots.

GAME 97:

WORD AT A TIME

Sometimes thinking of a complete sentence response can be too much. I get it.

If you can only muster one word, you're still not out of the conversation game.

You can still play your way into the conversation.

A crowd favorite improv game is Word at a Time Story. Players can only say one word. Then the next player says the next word. And on and on. The aim is to actually tell a cohesive story, and not disintegrate into chaotic jibber-jabber.

So you only have to respond with one word in this game. You can't just repeat a word, because this lesson is about and-ing and adding. The one word should add something new to what's already been said instead of just recapping.

Maybe someone says that garbage day was Tuesday, but no one ever took the trash away yesterday. Maybe you don't care about this conversation at all. It doesn't matter. You still need to let it go where it goes.

Now, you can't just say "garbage" or "Tuesday." That's recapping. It kind of shows you were maybe listening, but it doesn't move things along. Words that might move things forward would be "holiday" or "strike" or "problem."

When you only say one word, your word has a lot of heft. The other person has to decipher what you're talking about. They have to read between the lines, or word, and really do the heavy lifting. But for this game, that's okay.

Just add a word and volley it right back to the other person.

It's human nature to try to make it work. You just have to show you're trying.

GAME 98:

FREE ASSOCIATION

"Bug, insect, crawl, baby, stroller, stroll, walk, run, race, car."

I just free-associated!

Now, free association is fun on its own. You can certainly play this with friends and have a swell time. Just say the first thing that comes to mind based on the word they say. Just no repeating words!

But I want to keep our 120 games more connected to our daily grinds.

So let's free-associate more conversationally.

All you have to say is "that reminds me of . . ." or "that makes me think of . . ."

Maybe someone says, "My kid got called into the principal's office. He's always in trouble."

You could say, "That reminds me of a time I got in trouble."

Now, this example wouldn't be great in real life. The first person clearly has more to say about her kid getting in trouble.

So before you free-associate the conversation to a different place, try to let old topics exhaust themselves.

Let's try again.

Let's say this same woman has told the entire story of her kid getting in trouble. She doesn't know what to do. She's so tired. Then there's a pause. You don't know what to say, and she is done talking about her son's incident. Now would be a good time to free-associate.

"That reminds me of when you got in trouble." Or "That makes me think of how I got pulled over yesterday."

Now we're getting somewhere.

So the next time someone runs out of conversational steam

and you don't know where to go next, just free-associate. Don't worry about where it will take you.

Ooooh, that reminds me of the next game.

GAME 99:

GIFTED

Another way to think about anding people is what improvisers call gifts. I'm gonna try a sports metaphor again, so bear with. Gifts to improv are what assists are to basketball. They're like the set to the spike in volleyball.

Instead of worrying about saying awesome, life-alteringly amazing things, you want to be the assist person. You want to set up someone else to spike that ball.

Okay, no more sports. I'm exhausted.

Gifts give your real-life scenes somewhere to go. They give the person you're talking to some conversational fodder.

Let's say your neighbor is writing a screenplay. You always struggle with small talk with this particular neighbor, but today is different because today, you're Gifted. When he starts talking about how hot it is today, you're going to surprise him with a gift! Ask him how the screenplay is going.

This is going to get him talking and talking, and it's going to give you lots of new information that you can turn into more gifts in the future.

Let's say your colleague always sits in silence during lunch, but you for sure know she loves watching funny cat videos on YouTube. Give her a gift! Tell her about that cat you had once that always drank from a human glass on your nightstand. Hilarious. You know she's going to have a lot to talk about for the next hour, because cats.

To play Gifted, I'm going to need you to give at least three gifts today. Don't be stingy and don't expect anything in return.

Be the Santa Claus of small talk.

Ho ho ho.

GAME 100:

HOTSPOT

My favorite game for building confidence and trust in your teammates is probably Hotspot.[2] It's terrifying to play, but the payoff is money. Not literal money. The payoff is actually that you will feel more confident and creative and carefree, which is better than money.

One version of Hotspot goes like this. Everyone stands in a circle. Then one person goes to the center. That person gets a suggestion—a word or phrase—from the rest of the players. They are in the "hotspot," so they have to sing a song based on the suggestion. The aim of the game is really for the people standing in the circle to jump in and rescue the hotspot person by trading places with them and singing their own song that the previous song made them think of. Everyone is supposed to be supportive by singing and dancing along, so the hotspot person doesn't feel like such a tool.

Now I want you to make the universe your own personal game of Hotspot. No more worrying about what you're going to say next or whether or not the conversation is going well. In this game, you're in the hotspot, and it's your job to keep the conversation moving forward.

I want you to imagine you're in the hotspot. Let's say your coworkers are all talking about ants. You don't know much about ants, but you're in the hotspot, so you have to pull your weight! Now let's say your coworker says, "All I know is that we can't get rid of the ants in our kitchen. I'm not sure why they're such a problem this year."

You gotta jump in now! You're in the hotspot! You could say, "Yeah, ants are the worst! I do like how they can carry way more than their body weight. I can't do that. The last time I went to the gym was two years ago. I do like how gym memberships are covered by our insurance plan, though. That's pretty great."

Don't ask questions. Just keep riffing. Give the other person some dead air every now and again and see if they want to jump back in. In the above example, you really brought up three different topics. That's amazing! Your coworker could talk about ants more. (I hope they don't.) Or they could talk about working out, or gyms, or health insurance.

You are giving the people options.

And we all need options.

And that's the magic of and. It gives us more options, more things to build off.

It's not enough to just yes something. The and is what's going to give us the material to really create something with someone else.

That something could be a transcendent conversation about ants or it could be a good laugh.

"And" will help you bring more to the conversational table, regardless of what other people are dishing out.

But to bring the most to every table we're at, we need to care way less about making mistakes.

And that brings us to the next lesson.

TIME-OUT:
LET'S TALK ABOUT GETTING
SOME PROFESSIONAL HELP

I hope you aren't under the impression that I think these 120 games can cure mental illness. I don't think that for one second. That's why we need to talk about getting some professional help.

I want to talk about therapy. Especially before we embark on the last two lessons, I want to encourage you to seek therapy if you have any inclination to do so. These games are all in good fun, but they're not a remedy for an actual mental illness, so please talk to a professional if it's right for you.

I've gone to therapy numerous times in my life and always found it illuminating to talk out how my past was affecting my present. Without that insight, these games can only do so much.

Talk to a friend, a church leader, a relative. Just don't go it alone. I know we started these games with some lonely, hug-a-tree-type shit, but now that we're mixing and mingling and small-talking, a lot of personal baggage can come up. I want you to be able to call the hotline or go to the center if you need to talk.

We all need connection, and for many these games can help with that, but I don't want you to rely only on these games for your connection. I want you to therapy up, strengthen your circle of close friends, and reach out to the people who can help you process any difficulties that you're going through.

So please, please, please, don't be embarrassed or ashamed about your depression, your anxiety, your addiction, your mistakes, your past. Instead, pick up the phone and get the help you need.

Make that connection, so you can proceed.

LESSON 11
Sucking and Loving It
(Embracing Mistakes)

We've talked about how you aren't special. We've talked about how everyone else, except you, is a genius. We've even talked about how judgmental and egotistical you can be!

Maybe you were hoping the next lesson would be all about how far you've come. Maybe you thought I'd be doling out gold stars and blue ribbons just for playing.

Nope, not at all!

I think I have another way to make you feel better.

You suck. But you need to learn how to love it.

That's right. You are imperfect. I think I've made it perfectly clear just how imperfect I am. I've told you about my perfectionism, my anxiety, and my rage.

Now, I don't know what your deal is, but I'm 100 percent positive that you aren't perfect either.

Maybe you're clumsy or bad with money. Maybe you don't floss enough or vacuum too often. Maybe you're a bad listener or you can't sit still.

The good news is that perfection is impossible. The definition of perfection is different, anyway, depending on who you ask. But trust me, we all miss the mark every single day of our lives.

If you put yourself out into the world, you're going to mess up. If you try, you're going to fail sometimes.

So repeat after me: "I suck, but I love it. Mistakes are just miracles waiting to be born."

Now, let's start playing some games that will help you get comfortable with your mistakes and even start to make them work for you instead of against you.

GAME 101:

BABY ZOO

Now, I don't want you to create a literal zoo of babies. That's absolutely unethical on multiple levels. Instead, I'm asking you to see babies in a new light.

For this game, all you have to do is some field research. Next time you're around a toddler, let's say ages one to four, really watch their mistake-making process.

What do they do when they fall down? Babies fall down all the time! How do they handle it? How would you?

What do they do when they say something silly and people laugh at them? How do they react? How would you?

What happens when they try something beyond their current abilities? What happens immediately? What happens five minutes later? How would you handle putting yourself out there and failing?

I don't want to tell you the answers here. I really want you to make your observations and learn the lessons from the babies themselves.

For some reason, we're always trying to make babies be more like adults. Sometimes that's good, like teaching them how to walk and poop in toilets and drive cars. But in terms of making mistakes, babies know their shit.

Learn from the masters.

And remember, the moment we stop making mistakes is the moment we stop learning and improving.

A baby taught me that.

GAME 102:

MISTAKE TREES

It's arts and crafts time, y'all!

I want you to think of five so-called mistakes you've made in your life. Choose a variety of mistakes, old and new.

Now we're going to make Mistake Trees. I just want you to take some pretty paper and pretty markers, some glue or tape and scissors, and you're going to create one Mistake Tree for each of your five mistakes. It's like a cause-and-effect tree, but for mistakes.

Let's say you peed your pants in front of your biggest crush when you were fifteen. You could write it out on top of one of your pretty pieces of paper—"Peed Pants"—or you could use some clip art or draw a picture. Maybe a picture would be a mistake for this particular mistake, but hey, then you've got another tree to make. So carry on.

Now draw a line from you peeing and connect it with whatever happened as a result of your mistake. Maybe your crush left early. Then another line and event. Maybe he never spoke to you again. Then you met your future husband. Then you had a great wedding and now have two cute kids! That's your Mistake Tree!

Now, not all Mistake Trees end in glory, but I want you to create a visual for the actual results of your mistakes. Sometimes mistakes don't have a discernible payoff, but I'm pretty confident the majority of your trees won't be so bad.

GAME 103:

AWESOME SAUCE FLAWS

Do you still have that journal we discussed? Great.

No? Write this on a bar napkin, then. Or whatever you have handy.

This can be a lonely game. I've been asking you to mix and mingle with people for a few lessons now, and if you're anything like me, this can be depleting. It can be tough.

So put on those pj's and grab your journal, lonely girl. It's time to write it out.

I want you to list as many of your flaws and mistakes as you can think of. Be hard on yourself. Leave no stone unturned as you brainstorm all the reasons you suck.

Come up with at least ten. Your hair is always messy. You're always late. You lied to your wife. You spelled "parachute" wrong in your third-grade spelling bee, which led to a weak third-place finish.

Brainstorming a list of flaws and mistakes helped me think of that last one, which is one of my real-life missteps that I haven't thought about in at least two decades.

That's the point of meditating on your foibles. It will allow you to unearth long lost ways you don't measure up.

After your "you suck" list seems complete and you're thoroughly depressed, fear not! You're going to turn those flaws into fantastic.

The next step of this game is to go through your list and put a positive spin on each negative.

Let's try it using our same examples as before.

Your hair is always messy? You don't waste time on your hair because you spend it on caring for your family. And besides, you're not vain or egotistical.

You're always late? You have a full calendar. You are full

of life and burning the candle at both ends. You're a busy bee with a lot of friends and responsibilities.

You lied to your wife? How dare you! No, no, no, let's give even this one a fair shake at a positive slant. You love your wife. You don't want to hurt her. You're doing your best. Today you're a better person than before. You are getting better every day!

You spelled "parachute" wrong in 1988? They've since invented spell-check. Eventually, you will have editors or pay friends in white wine to edit your bad spelling. You don't ever want to jump out of a plane, so there's no need to know how to spell "parachute" anyway.

This game is about putting your flaws and mistakes in perspective. Sure, we could let them tell our whole story. We could let them be bigger than life.

Or we could see the other side, the side where they're just one little piece of who we are. We can obsess about what makes us suck.

Or we can keep it moving and be awesome anyway.

Be awesome.

GAME 104:

EVERYONE SAW THAT

I don't know about you, but whenever I see someone trip, slip, or fall, I look the other way. I pretend like I didn't notice them fucking up. I mean, I might not laugh about it till later . . . but I for sure saw it.

Well, that ends today.

The next time you see someone making a mistake, I want you to kindly acknowledge it. They are a human—fallible, and messy—just like you. Celebrate their humanity with them by pointing out their screwup.

A woman trips on the curb? You could say, "Oooops, stupid curb. You okay?"

Your teacher spells "parachute" wrong? Don't pretend it didn't happen. Raise your hand and say, "I'm not a spelling bee champ or anything, but your 'parachute' spelling isn't doing it for me."

The point here is certainly not to embarrass anyone. That would defeat the whole purpose of this game. The point is to celebrate their attempt, to empathize and connect with someone because they make mistakes just like you.

This game will also help you see that mistakes are happening all around you, all the time. When we pretend they aren't, we're trying to create a perfect world that just doesn't exist. We're trying to make the mistake-maker feel better by pretending they didn't make a mistake. This isn't super helpful because they did make a mistake, and they definitely saw you seeing it happen. You're missing an opportunity to connect when you pretend someone is perfect. Because they're not, just like you're not.

So point that shit out!

GAME 105:

FESS UP

Speaking of pointing out mistakes, I want you to start pointing out your own as well.

I want you to think back on some mistakes you've made in your day, and I want you to fess up.

Admitting our mistakes can be quite liberating.

Start with some from your childhood.

I have one that's really crazy embarrassing. I shouldn't write about it here, but in the pursuit of letting go of the shame of our mistakes, here goes nothing.

When I was in third grade, I was staying inside for recess one day. This makes sense if you've ever met me. I'm not a recess guy. Some other students and I were helping the teacher clean the class aquarium. Then, all of the sudden, my stomach was not okay. I'm understating here. I was straight-up gonna poop my pants.

I asked if I could use the restroom. The moment I walked into the bathroom is when things really took a turn for the worse. I didn't poop my pants, but, unfortunately, I also didn't quite make it to the toilet. There was 100 percent doo-doo on the ground. I tried to clean it as best I could with toilet paper. Thirty years later, I still remember sweating profusely at the thought of anyone ever finding out what had just happened. But instead of cleaning the mess, the toilet paper just kind of smeared stuff around and made it worse. I accidentally made it look like there was a caca vandal on the loose!

After recess, another teacher came into class and whispered something in my teacher's ear. My teacher's face dropped. I knew she had just heard about some poopy on the floor of the boys' room. She announced that someone had done a very bad thing. They had purposefully made a mess in the bathroom.

I was pretty sure everyone could tell it was me. I turned neon red and continued to sweat profusely at the thought of being found out.

But I was never caught. I took my mistake and buried it. I turned it into a painful secret that still makes me incredibly sweaty just thinking about.

But after revealing it in the pages of this book, it no longer feels like it controls or defines me. I mainly just feel really bad for the ashamed and extremely embarrassed and scared little Clay.

So that's the game. Fess up to your past mistakes. Stop letting them define and control you.

It will also humanize you. We tend to empathize with people who make mistakes because we also make shit tons of them ourselves. Sorry, I couldn't resist the poo pun.

More about shitting on the floor in the next lesson (wow, this book really took a turn), but for now, let's keep playing some games that will help us with the ancient art of fucking up.

GAME 106:

SORRY, NOT SORRY

One of my earliest bad habits was profuse over-apologizing. After the slightest mistake, I would say, "Sorry, I'm sorry, sorry, sorry, I'm really sorry, sorry."

Then my mom would tell me not to apologize so much.

And I would say sorry.

I didn't want to deal with the fact that I wasn't perfect, that I'd messed up, or that I had disappointed someone. I didn't want to deal with that yucky embarrassed feeling of not getting everything just right.

And so I apologized.

This is a bad habit. Apologizing is a way to try to sweep those mistakes under the proverbial rug.

No more sweeping! We're owning our mistakes from here on out.

So the next time you apologize for a little misstep, you get one strike.

Two strikes for the second apology.

And then three strikes, you're out for that third sorry.

And if you mess up this game, it's cool. Just start over when you get three strikes.

Try not to apologize for those stupid, little mistakes.

Big mistakes that hurt people? Definitely apologize for those. But let the little ones go.

And even if you mess this game up royally, I'll still love you, you imperfect piece of mess, you.

GAME 107:

ACCIDENTALLY ON PURPOSE

It's one thing to fess up to old mistakes; it's another to make new mistakes on purpose.

That's exactly what I want you to do. You're going to make some small mistakes on purpose.

Think of some really harmless little mistakes. A little stumble, publicly spelling something wrong, using the wrong word, taking multiple attempts at parallel parking. Then, I want you to enact three of these fake mistakes today.

Notice how it makes you feel to purposely mess up. Does it get easier throughout the day? Why do you think messing up affects you this way?

It's good fun to pratfall, so enjoy your fake mistakes.

If you're feeling especially brave, you can up the ante. Let's think back to that game you might have played as a teenager. You're in a public place with your friends. Then someone has to yell something embarrassing, usually pertaining to genitals, as loud as they can. Then another friend tries to top that. It's like a game of chicken . . . only with yelling and genitals.

If you're feeling confident after your three little fake mistakes, I want you to really embarrass yourself. Think of something awkward you can yell out in public. It's like when you're talking to someone in a loud bar and the music suddenly stops, but you're still screaming about your strange itchy rash. You want to recreate that kind of public embarrassment.

You could yell, "then she left me" or "discharge" or "subpoena." Get creative with it.

Teenagers are experimenting with identity and reputation all the time. It's why they test the limits of their own embarrassment and rebelliousness.

Then we get old and stop messing with that discomfort as much as possible.

I think it's another missed opportunity.

Keep feeling alive.

Keep being embarrassed.

Keep yelling "penis."

I hope all this purposeful messing up helps you later when you accidentally miss the mark . . . or the toilet.

Embarrassment is normal and natural.

So play around with the limits of yours.

GAME 108:

DAD JOKES

Sometimes I think I have a child for the sole purpose of being able to tell dad jokes freely and openly.

Dad jokes are bad jokes. They're heavy on puns. Usually, they result in an eye roll or a groan. This is how you know that the dad joke is working.

That's why dad jokes are perfect for getting over our own shyness and embarrassment.

So for this game, get those dad jokes ready. I don't care if you google "dad jokes" and just recycle someone else's punny punch line. Just get some dad jokes ready to go.

Some classics are "What animal can jump higher than a tree? Trees can't jump!" and "Did you hear about the new restaurant on the moon? The food is good, just no atmosphere." I think you get the idea. They're just cringy, bad jokes.

When you find yourself in your next small group, try out one of your dad jokes. Try not to have any shame in your game. Don't apologize after the fact, and definitely don't preface your joke by saying you're going to tell a bad joke. Own it. Tell it proudly and confidently.

Because if there's one person who has no shame in their game about sounding lame . . .

. . . it's Dad.

GAME 109:

THAT'S WHAT HE SAID

I don't want to only give you games that force you to embarrass yourself. I'm a nice guy. Kind of.

I also want to give you a game to try to end your missteps with a flourish, to stick the landing, to go in grace.

I'm calling this one That's What He Said. The next time you say something stupid or just generally botch something in public, I want you to have a little, jokey phrase that puts a button on your mistake. I want you to tada that shit, point out the fact that you messed up, and then own it with a punch line.

One way is to just say, "That's what he said," after you screw something up. Will it make sense? Nine times out of ten it won't. Doesn't matter.

You slip on the sidewalk. "That's what he said."

You say "irregardless" instead of "regardless." "That's what he said." That one could slightly make sense.

You call someone Anna instead of Elsa. "That's what he said." Actually, that one might also make sense in certain contexts.

That's it. It's simple.

Own your shit.

You could also put a button on your next mistake by saying, "And then I found five dollars." My friends taught me this one, because I'm a notoriously bad storyteller. I lose the point of a story midway through. Sometimes, I forget what I was even going to say in the first place. So some friends taught me to just end with, "And then I found five dollars." This way, no matter how off track I get, it feels like my story has some kind of an ending. A happy one, too. Finding any number of dollars is always thrilling.

So you could also end your next mistake with "And then I found five dollars."

Forget to put the towels away? "And then I found five dollars."

Lock your keys in your car? "And then I found five dollars."

Walk into the wrong classroom? "And then I found five dollars."

I know it may seem like this one will just exacerbate your embarrassment, but since owning our mistakes is our primary goal, I'm still here for it.

You can also make up your own catchphrase that you use after you screw something up.

"Who's driving this thing?"

"Who put that there?"

"Where are we?"

This will make mistake-making something to look forward to.

And besides, in the sitcom of life, everyone needs a good catchphrase.

GAME 110:

SPECIAL ANNOUNCEMENT

Our lesson on messing up ends with another chance for you to put yourself on the spot.

Too many times, we play it safe. We blend in. We do whatever we can to go unnoticed.

This saves us from embarrassment, sure.

But it also saves us from reaching our ultimate greatness.

So I want you to put yourself in the hot seat. I want you to speak up before you have any idea what you're going to say. This is the danger—and thrill—of improv. I want you to put yourself in the position of having no idea what's going to come babbling out of your mouth.

The next time you're in a group, just say that you have an important announcement or toast or story. Just blurt it out.

"I have an announcement!"

This only works if you truly have nothing to say. It's not risky if you have it all planned out. Then it's just an announcement, like the old, boring kind of announcement.

Without a thought in your pretty little head, just blab out, "I'd like to make a toast!"

Then just start talking! Figure it out as you go.

Or "Everyone, listen up! I have a story for all of you!"

Again, this only works if you have zero stories to tell at that moment.

Make it up on the spot.

If things get hairy, look around the room and get inspired by what you're seeing. "I've known Mark and Sam for twenty years. We met when we were all in grad school . . ."

You know how you met. Just tell it!

More often than not, I stand on the sidelines at gatherings. You know, behind the grandfather clock. I envy people who can take center stage and deliver an impromptu message. The only way we can begin to get off the sidelines is if we put ourselves in the position to take a risk and mess up royally.

It doesn't matter how prepared you are or whether or not you know what you're going to say. What matters is that you got off the sidelines and put yourself out there.

Plus, if it goes really badly, that's just another story for the next time you yell, "I have an announcement!"

And so it goes with mistakes. We have to put ourselves in perceived harm's way in order to start dealing with our insecurities, shame, and embarrassment.

Which brings us to our final lesson. In improv, as in life, you gotta go big or go home. You gotta make big choices. You gotta shit in the middle of the floor.

LESSON 12

Shit in the Middle of the Floor

(Making Big Choices)

Improv works when people are bold and committed to their choices. You have to be really clear when you fold the pretend towels or work the pretend jackhammer. Then your partner jumps right in, saving you from the embarrassment of doing pretend things all by your lonesome.

Which show would you want to watch? Someone jumps out onstage excitedly. They start spinning their arms wildly and saying, "Swoosh." Their scene partner doesn't know what they're doing, but they run out anyway and start swooshing with their partner.

Now for option B. Two people walk out onstage meekly. They each just stand there waiting for the other one to do something.

One hundred percent of the time, I pick option A! Someone

did something! It was exciting to watch because they went for it. They committed to a big choice. Who cares if things work out or not? The fun part was just seeing some bold choices and some conviction.

You can probably guess by now that I feel the same way about life. I mean, it's a cliché that you have to play to win, or that you lose all the games you don't play, or whatever. But it's a cliché because there's truth to it. You have to try big and sometimes fail big in order to get the most out of life. I didn't say, "in order to win," because that doesn't always happen. But I don't think that's the point anyway. I think the point is showing up in a big way, putting yourself out there, trying new things, failing, getting up, and then making more big, bold, beautiful choices.

When I taught acting at a university, I would call making big choices "shitting in the middle of the floor." I like the phrase maybe because I shat on the floor in third grade. Maybe it was an unconscious thing. Or maybe because it exemplifies making big choices. I mean, there's not a lot of choices bigger than shitting in the middle of the floor.

So I invite you now to really show up and make the biggest choices you can muster as we round out our twelve lessons.

GAME 111:

WORST-CASE SCENARIO

What's the worst thing that could happen? Isn't that the thing your well-intentioned friend sometimes asks when you consider taking a risk?

I'm here to tell you that your friend is totally onto something.

Before we start making those bodacious, big, ballsy choices, we need to make sure we know that nine times out of ten, the worst-case scenario ain't that bad.

The next time you catch yourself flirting with a big choice, I want you to literally list the absolute worst things that could happen.

If you're thinking about applying for a new job, your current boss could find out and fire you and you might not get the new job. That's definitely not good news, but it's not the end of the world, either.

Let's say you want to ask a guy out. Worst-case scenario is he says no and laughs in your face and tells all his friends how absurd you asking him out is. You're still in one piece, yes?

Maybe you want to write a book. It might never get published, or it will and people will think it sucks.

Now go through and list the benefits of trying.

Applying for a new job keeps you fresh. It allows you to network and see what else is out there.

Asking someone out means you might get to go on a date,

maybe meet the love of your life, at least not sit at home eating TV dinners with the cat.

And writing a book helps you process your thoughts. I wrote a memoir that never saw the light of day, but it helped me deal with my dad dying and some lingering unhealthy decision-making. I'm glad I wrote it.

Writing this book has allowed me to practice walking the walk when it comes to the mental benefits of improv. Meditating on the ideas helps me enact them on a daily basis, and I know it will help others, so I'm glad I wrote it, even if you think it sucks.

Just list the worst-case scenarios and the benefits of trying.

I think what you'll notice is that making big choices isn't as risky as it initially seems.

And the possible payoff almost always makes it worth it.

Remember that improv scene with the wild-armed, swooshing guy? I'd be that guy over someone stuck on the sidelines any day.

GAME 112:

CHOOSE CHOICE

I'm a Libra, so I usually sacrifice having an opinion to preserve social harmony.

I'm also a Midwesterner, and we tend to avoid confrontation like we avoid our emotions.

It's true that having a preference can sometimes lead to conflict, but it's also equally true that having a preference is the first step in making those big, bold choices. You have to give a shit about something before you can do something big.

So I want you to Choose Choice.

Anytime someone asks what you want to eat tonight, have a preference.

Anytime someone asks where you want to hang out, have a preference.

Anytime someone asks you what you want to do this weekend, have a preference.

I think you get the idea. You just need to Choose Choice.

Don't be that person who always says "whatever." You need to get in the habit of choosing.

And the more you choose, the more you're priming yourself for big things, you know, like shitting on floors.

GAME 113:

BREAK THE ROUTINE

When you're a grown-up-type person, it's easy to get stuck in a routine. We have to go to work. We have to wake up in the morning and get ready to go to work. We have to come home from work when we're done working. It gets monotonous.

It's time to break up that routine, even just a little.

All you need to do is make a different choice than you

normally would. If you normally have a salad for lunch, have a burger. If you normally go the quickest way Waze tells you, try the scenic route. If you always come home and watch TV, try going for a jog or painting some shit.

Break your routine three times in one day for the win.

What do you win?

A little more joie de vivre and a whole lot of nothing. Again, these are make-pretend games where you don't win anything tangible.

But winning joie de vivre isn't that bad.

No shame in needing to google joie de vivre. I had to google how to spell it. Plus, I still think you're devastatingly fantastic.

GAME 114:

NARNIA COCO CHANEL

I heard once . . . somewhere . . . that Coco Chanel said that you should take off one accessory before leaving the house. I think she was trying to make people more chic, like we tend to overdo it or something.

I say pooh-pooh, Coco. More is more.

We're practicing being bold, so let's turn Coco on her head. Let's put on an extra something or other before we strut out that front door.

Put on an extra belt, a second purse, a fascinator, an extra layer, a shawl, a ribbon, jewelry. Get creative with it.

We worry too much about blending in and matching and being on trend. No more.

Express yourself. Turn some heads. Put on one extra item before strutting down that runway we call life.

GAME 115:

WORK THE ROOM

As I've previously stated, I'm not so good at networking or mingling or just generally being in public places. I can't small-talk to save my life, so maybe this game is more for me than for anyone else.

But I hope it forces you out into the middle of the party, too.

The next time you're at a mixer or a cocktail hour or wedding or what have you, you have to chat up at least three people.

Just prance right up to someone and start talking. "Where are you coming from this evening?" "What are you drinking?" "How do you know the bride and groom?" That's one way to earn your three chat-ups.

Or you can have a little more fun with it. "Rank your top three desserts in order." "What's in your refrigerator right now?" "If you were a cartoon character, which one would you be?" Now you're having some fun with it and getting bolder. You earn an extra ten points, which means nothing.

The real winning is that you got out there and met some new people, and that might just change your life.

And all it took was jumping in there and asking some randos some rando questions.

GAME 116:

DO THE DAMN THING

I have a long list of things that I would love to do but haven't gotten around to. I have at least five more books I plan on writing. I have a list of places I'd love to visit. I have companies I want to start and people I want to ask to help me. Sometimes I avoid returning phone calls or running certain errands. A general anxiety or a massive fear of rejection or failure holds me back.

Don't be like me.

I want you to make a list of all the big and small things you've been putting off.

You could use that journal of yours or just make a list any old place.

Then you simply have to do one of those things.

That's it! Just Do the Damn Thing.

I think you'll be surprised at how it makes you feel to cross something major off your list. I think you'll want to do more of the things you've been avoiding. And I think you'll begin to see that putting yourself out there can be its own reward.

Or you'll just get one thing accomplished, which is still a victory in my book.

GAME 117:

HOT DATE

When I tell people I sometimes go to restaurants, bars, and even clubs by myself, they're usually horrified.

It can seem pretty scary to go out into the world alone.

Take away the crutches of cell phones, alcohol, smoking, and even reading a book, and suddenly going on a date with yourself sounds like a horror film!

But that's what I want you to do. Face whatever negative emotions emerge as you sit there . . . alone.

You might think everyone is judging you or that people think you're a loser or the bartender thinks you're a creeper. You might feel uncomfortable or anxious. I want you to pay close attention to these feelings, because they're the same feelings that are causing you to stay on the sidelines and not make big, bold, beautiful choices in life.

Start small. Just take yourself out for a coffee. Then build up to a full dinner and walk through the park.

I hope you get more used to putting yourself out into the world without the distractions of technology or other people.

I hope you start to see what feelings are stopping you from shitting in the middle of the floor.

I hope you have a really lovely time on your Hot Date with yourself.

GAME 118:

GO TO SOMEWHERE

I'm going to need you to get out of the house, friend. Now, you don't have to go to the South of France or scale the Great Wall or whatever, but you do need to get out more.

See the world!

This game couldn't be simpler.

All you have to do is go to one new place today. Of course you could plan some sort of *Eat, Pray, Love* or *How Stella Got Her Groove Back* globe-trotting, but, at least for this game, you could also just go to the new bakery that opened on Main Street.

It could be a part of the park you've never been or a corner store that you usually don't go to.

It could be some place you found online or somewhere a friend suggested.

The point is, keep your ears open for new place ideas, and then go to that new place!

We have only so many days on this planet. The least we can do is add in some spatial variety.

I always feel better when I Go to Somewhere new.
I hope you do, too.

GAME 119:

GOOGLE IT

I've heard that working for Google is this fantastic experience where you eat all kinds of cool foods for free. I also heard that they encourage their employees to spend 10 percent of their time working on their dream projects. That's 10 percent of their time on what might be pipe dreams that won't pan out.

So let's be like Google. Let's Google It.

Do I want you to eat cool foods? Sure, why not?

But I mainly want you to spend at least 10 percent of your time on what may be just your pipe dream, on your speculative life play. Spend one-tenth of your day laboring away on that project that might not turn into anything anyone gives a shit about.

Write the book, produce the musical, make your own soap, learn the piano, take the night class, learn dog whispering, buy some stocks.

Whatever it is that gets you going, that's what I want you to do 10 percent of the time. It's not enough time to sink your ship, but it will be plenty of time to get you excited about life again.

And don't think about where your project is going.

Just enjoy the time you get to spend doing it.

GAME 120:

SISTERHOOD OF THE TRAVELING ARTICLE OF CLOTHING

When I was single, a group of my best friends and I started a little game based on that *Sisterhood of the Traveling Pants* film. If I'm being honest, that film is everything, and it makes me cry profusely—not like the ending of *Pocahontas*, but still legit waterworks.

Our game was a way to challenge each other to take bigger risks. We called it "The Sisterhood of the Traveling Jockstrap," and we were challenging each other to be more courageous when it came to love, sex, and relationships. Some of our individual challenges were to talk to someone at a bar, to go on three dates with the same person, and to have a threesome. I'm not saying which was my challenge, but I think you get the general idea.

We all had very different goals, but that didn't matter. The game helped keep everyone accountable and motivated to reach their goal. Whenever someone reached their goal, they got to keep the traveling jockstrap until the next person achieved their goal.

I stand by this game. Of course you and your friends don't have to have slutty goals or use a traveling jockstrap, but the general idea of the game still holds up as a good motivator.

Choose a group you want to play this game with. Then

choose the article of clothing you want to be your traveling article of clothing. It's more fun when you try to make it symbolic, adorned, and somehow special. Then sit down together and go over your individual goals. These goals should be challenging to attain. They should take you out of your comfort zone. Remember, we're trying to make really big, shit-on-floor choices here.

Then you simply hold each other accountable for your goals and check in with each other periodically on your progress. Like a jockstrap, support each other. When someone reaches their goal, they get the article of clothing. It makes it more fun if that person puts some kind of symbolic decoration onto the article of clothing before they pass it along again. When you reach your goal, you can always stay in the game by setting a new goal.

Make sure the group doesn't allow easy goals. This game only works if each person is taking a risk of some kind. And risk is different depending on the person. For some people, a threesome is risky business. For others, it's Tuesday night. Only you and your friends know your comfort zone and what it would mean to step out of it.

None of the other lessons matter if we can't jump onto that stage in the first place. So be brave and don't overthink it as you step out of your personal comfort zone.

AFTERWORD

Improv has always been a way for me to let go of my anxiety—to jump onstage, stop overthinking, and just play. I've always wanted my real life to have more of that improv feel, and this book is my way of bringing that to my own life and to yours.

I've been researching and writing about improv's effects on the mind for a decade. This book has been my first attempt to take everything I know and make it completely accessible and usable for everyone.

I think it would be hypocritical to write a really polished and perfect book about taking big risks and not being afraid to make mistakes, so I've tried to live the improv spirit in even the writing of this book. I never dreamed I would mention defecation or Kim Kardashian so many times, but here we are.

Improv isn't perfect. Life is messy.

Letting our guard down and not overthinking with our conscious brains allows our unsightly unconscious to do the talking. And that can lead to . . . well, in my case, shit and Kardashians.

But I think there's value in letting this underused unconscious brain do more of the heavy lifting. Unlike the conscious brain, the unconscious is never depleted. No matter how tired or zoned out I am, my unconscious brain can still do its creative thang. Not so with the conscious brain. It takes a lot of energy to work our conscious brains. It's why I struggle to write at night and why you should do the most creative, brain-intensive tasks first thing in the morning. Conscious thought is freakin' exhausting.

Our culture seems to overvalue conscious thought. We overthink and overplan and worry and regret. I hope you've been able to step out of this way of thinking just a bit by playing the improv-inspired games in each of the twelve lessons.

Let's recap.

First, we started with a blank stage. Then, we set it. We did this by trying to clear our heads and start with an open mind and heart.

Second, we calmed the hell down. We learned some breathing and visualization games that helped us relax and de-escalate.

Third, we tried to get playful by gamifying our everyday lives. We played games that spoke to the child within.

Fourth, we played around with getting more positive. Negativity has no place in improv, and it's also no fun to be around in real life, so we aimed to kill Debbie Downer once and for all.

Fifth, we addressed our judginess. Improv doesn't work when we're judging our fellow players, and real life doesn't work as well when we're judging . . . everyone else.

Sixth, we began to see others as the geniuses, poets, and

artists they truly are. We have to think the world of others in order for our real-life scenes to be positive, collaborative experiences.

Seventh, we busted the myth that we were ever special in the first place. We are just one of billions, no more or less special than any other human being on the planet. How's that for fun?

Eighth, we played games to improve our listening. Most people think they're good listeners. Most people are wrong. But now that you played those ten games, you're not most people.

Ninth, we played games based on the Yes part of improv's "Yes, And" rule. We worked on agreeing with others instead of shooting down their realities or getting defensive.

Tenth, we added the And to "Yes, And." Real-life scenes don't go anywhere when no one adds new information.

Eleventh, we played games to make us face our embarrassment demons. We all make mistakes, and embracing them is what helps us be more present and relatable.

Finally, twelfth, we played ten games to help us live life to the fullest and make big, bold, beautiful choices every day.

With so many people so plugged into social media and all other media, it's easy to get bogged down in thinking that everyone else is perfect, that everyone else is living their best life, that you just don't stack up. People present their idealized selves on social media—perfect abs, perfect lighting, perfect makeup, perfect children, perfect job.

I think you know by now that I'm definitely not perfect, but these games continue to help me slow down, stop spiraling, and mix and mingle with the people around me. Every single day I wake up and make a decision to play my way sane. Do I still want to scream when people are hogging the sidewalk? Sometimes. But I turn it into a game and pretend I'm an alien. Suddenly, I don't want to scream quite so much. Do I still want to hide behind grandfather clocks to avoid talking to strangers? For sure. But I fight the urge and make it a game. Then, I'm chatting and learning new things about the people around me, instead of fretting and sweating. Do I still assume my boss wants to fire me and my husband wants a divorce, and I'll for sure die penniless, old, and alone? Not as much as I used to. These games have helped me make a new habit of asking for clarification and figuring out what people are actually saying, instead of always assuming the worst. Games have allowed me to get out of my head and become more present and connected with others.

It's more important than ever to take the twelve improv lessons and apply them to our everyday lives. We have no idea what the hell is going to happen in the future. No one has a crystal ball or a Magic 8-Ball or any other balls that can tell the future. There could be more pandemics, natural disasters, and recessions. People could lose it all. Hell, we could all die tomorrow, but I'd much rather calm down and enjoy the moment while I still can. We can never get rid of uncertainty, but playing our way sane helps us stop worrying about the things we can't change and start enjoying the awesome things that are already going on.

You're not perfect. No one is, but when we approach others with open hearts, have fun, stay positive, stop judging, treat people like geniuses, reduce our own egos, actively listen, find points of agreement, add onto ideas, embrace mistakes, and make bold choices, we're at least starting with all the ingredients for an incredible, collaborative interaction.

And that's all improv can do, really. I can't tell you that every exchange you have will be perfect now that you've read this book. Of course it won't.

But anyone who has seen an improv show knows that not all improvised scenes are perfect. That's not the point at all. Not one bit.

The point is that we can practice getting our real-life scenes off to a good start by playing these 120 improv-inspired games. And when you do this with humility and an open heart and mind, even the fuckups will be better because you'll have more people on your team, more people who have your back.

And there's a lot of power in having people's backs.

And there's limitless possibilities in having your own.

I got your back, and trust that playing your way through these twelve lessons will help you open up, self-reflect, make bigger choices, and get more creative and collaborative as you step out into the world each day and play your way sane.

ACKNOWLEDGMENTS

I want to thank Emily Carleton and Leila Campoli for making this book possible. They are the absolute dream team. Emily, besides having the literal best taste in films, you've been the best collaborator I could have asked for. You took a chance on an irreverent book, and I'm thrilled to be on this journey with you. And Leila, you're my rock. You made me feel like there were no stupid questions, even when I was asking the legit stupidest questions. Thank you. I have a feeling this is only the beginning. Thanks also to the whole Stonesong family for being so welcoming to their newest member.

Without Robyn Curtis, my editor for *Theatrical Improvisation, Consciousness, and Cognition*, I would never have connected with Emily, and this book never would have happened. I'm indebted to you for allowing *Play Your Way Sane* to finally see the light of day.

Thank you to the entire team at Tiller Press and Simon & Schuster. Samantha Lubash, you were a miracle to work with—accessible and encouraging. Patrick Sullivan and Laura Levatino created a beautifully designed book that I can't take my eyes off of. Laura Flavin and Lauren Ollerhead helped get the word out. The entire Tiller Team—Annie Craig, Benjamin Holmes,

Acknowledgments

Allison Har-zvi, Theresa DiMasi, and Michael Anderson—made this a seamless and exciting experience for me.

I'm also extremely grateful to Sophia Taylor and Gabriel Smoller for helping me get my social media footing, Caleb Kenney and the Kelp Creative Agency for giving my website a much-needed makeover, and Max Flatow for the incredibly hot glamour shots.

I wouldn't have accumulated the ideas to create these games without all the incredible teachers I've had throughout my life. Thank you to Keith Johnstone and all my teachers, friends, and peers at the College of Wooster, Tufts, NYU, the Strasberg Institute, UCB, the Magnet, iO, and Second City. And thanks to the Don't Throw Shoes crew for introducing me to improv and starting me down this path in the first place.

Thank you to all my loyal www.playyourwaysane.com subscribers, aka Players. This noble experiment began online, and your early interest and enthusiasm were the catalysts for this book. To my editors Devon Frye at *Psychology Today* and Anna Chui at Lifehack, you both helped more people discover my writing about improv, science, and the everyday, and I'm so grateful for your early interest in and support of my writing.

Thanks to Ken Sims and Liz Dahmen for looking at early versions of this book and for inspiring me to keep going. And where would I be without my friends Mary Sabo, Mary Reynolds, Jim Beaudry, Rhiannon Fink, Nate Saete, Ryan Prado and Adam Deremer, Rachel Friedman and Adam Prentice, Don Love, Claybourne Elder and Eric Rosen, Kyle Field

Acknowledgments

and Thomas Recktenwald, JC Vasquez and Julien Blanchet, Whitney Fisch, Kate Jordan-Downs, Margi Hazlett, Katie Hammond, Josh Diaz, the High Meadow crew, and all my friendly neighbors, both literal and metaphoric?

In addition to shouting out the love and support of the entire Drinko/Silić family, I have to thank my mom, Debbie Drinko, for inspiring my playfulness for the last forty years and for being the ultimate cheerleader of my writing, and my sisters Kim and Bonnie, my OG playmates.

Thanks to my husband, Haris Silić, for giving me the consistency and security to be able to keep playing and dreaming, and for being the best Kris Jenner this Kim K could have asked for; and to my daughter, Ella, for reawakening my sense of awe and curiosity.

NOTES

Introduction

1. Quoted in Jeff Griggs, *Guru: My Days with Del Close* (Chicago: Ivan R. Dee, 2005).

Lesson 2:
Calm the Hell Down

1. Lee Strasberg, *A Dream of Passion: The Development of the Method* (New York: Plume 132, 1987), 84.

2. Ibid.

Lesson 4:
Killing Debbie Downer
(Getting and Staying Positive)

1. I played a version of the Yay Game at a Keith Johnstone workshop in Berlin, which I describe in Clay Drinko, *Theatrical Improvisation, Consciousness, and Cognition* (New York: Springer, 2013).

Lesson 5:
Thou Shalt Not Be Judgy

1. Keith Johnstone, *Impro: Improvisation and the Theatre* (Abingdon-on-Thames, UK: Routledge, 2012).

Lesson 6:
World of Geniuses

1. Quoted in Griggs, *Guru*.

2. Nicholas A. Coles, Jeff T. Larson, and Heather C. Lench, "A Meta-Analysis of the Facial Feedback Literature: Effects of Facial Feedback on Emotional Experience Are Small and Variable," *Psychological Bulletin* 145, no. 6 (2019): 610.

Lesson 7:
Your Mom Was Wrong
(You Aren't Special)

1. Steven Johnson, *Emergence: The Connected Lives of Ants, Brains, Cities, and Software* (New York: Simon & Schuster, 2002).

2. Viola Spolin and Paul Sills, *Improvisation for the Theater: A Handbook of Teaching and Directing Techniques* (Northwestern University Press, 1999).

3. Ibid.

4. Charna Halpern, Del Close, and Kim Johnson, *Truth in Comedy: The Manual of Improvisation* (Colorado Springs, CO: Meriwether Publishing, 1994).

Lesson 10:
And What?

1. Keith Johnstone, *Impro for Storytellers* (Abingdon-on-Thames, UK: Routledge, 2014).

2. Halpern, Close, and Johnson, *Truth in Comedy*.